Dean Forest & Wye Valley

A

Forestry Commission Guide

Dean Forest & Wye Valley

Edited by Herbert L. Edlin

London: Her Majesty's Stationery Office 1974

ISBN 0 11 710036 6

From *Lines* composed a few miles above Tintern Abbey, on revisiting *during a tour,* 1798:

Five years have past; five summers, with the length
Of five long winters! and again I hear
These waters, rolling from their mountain springs
With a soft inland murmur.—Once again
Do I behold these steep and lofty cliffs,
That on a wild secluded scene impress
Thoughts of more deep seclusion; and connect
The landscape with the quiet of the sky.
The day is come when I again repose
Here, under this dark sycamore, and view
These plots of cottage-ground, these orchard-tufts,
Which at this season, with their unripe fruits,
Are clad in one green hue, and lose themselves
'Mid groves and copses. Once again I see
These hedge-rows, hardly hedge-rows, little lines
Of sportive wood run wild: these pastoral farms,
Green to the very door; . . . . .
How oft, in spirit, have I turned to thee,
O sylvan Wye! thou wanderer thro' the woods,
How often has my spirit turned to thee!

Wordsworth

Contents

Acknowledgements

In addition to the authors whose names appear on the Contents page, the following contributors have assisted in the production of this Guide:

Text The staff of the Conservator of Forests for South West England, and the Conservator of Forests for South Wales, and in particular Messrs J. R. Hampson, A. Joslin, M. J. Dunn, B. G. Venner and B. G. Elley.

Cover Picture This is by Mr Charles Tunnicliffe, R.A. The scene is the River Wye below Symond's Yat, close to the Biblins, below the Seven Sisters Rocks of the Highmeadow Woods.

Drawings The frontispiece and the chapter headings are by Mr E.J. Rice who is Principal of the Lydney School of Art.

Photographs
Thanks are due to the following photographers for kindly providing the pictures listed below:
Frank Thompson, of Coleford, for plates 1–4, 8, 13, 17–19, 22–24, 31–34, 37, 39, 40, 42 and 52
Eagle Photos, Cheltenham, for plates 5, 7, 10, 11, 14, 15, 20, 50 and 51, mostly by Bill Bawden
Gerald Smith of Dean Forest Studios, Coleford, for plates, 6, 12, 16, 25, 29, 30, 38 and 41
B.V.Cave, of Mitcheldean, for plates 21, 56 and 57
Walter Scott, Bradford, for plate 26
Leonard and Marjorie Gayton, East Grinstead, for plates 27, 28, 35 and 49
Phillip Clarkson-Webb, of Aylburton, near Lydney, for plates 43–46
L. Starling, of Tidenham, near Chepstow, for plates 47, 48, 53–55 and 58

Maps These are reproduced from, or based on, the Ordnance Survey by kind permission of the Controller of Her Majesty's Stationery Office.
A.J.Drake provided details for the rambling maps. The geological maps are based on the work of Her Majesty's Geological Survey.

Verses by the Monmouthshire poet W. H. Davies are reproduced by kind permission of Mrs Davies and Messrs Jonathan Cape; that by Thomas Hardy by kind permission of Messrs MacMillans; and those by the Forest of Dean poet, F. W. Harvey, by kind permission of the author.

Badge of King Charles II, Carolus Rex II, on the Speech House, built in 1680

Foreword

The VII Earl of Radnor, KG, KCVO

The Royal Forest of Dean is one of the oldest and most valuable of
our national woodlands, and the Forestry Commissioners, as succes-
sors to the former Office of Woods and Forests, have always paid
close regard to their custodianship of this unique area. Likewise the
Highmeadow Woods, acquired by the nation in 1817, and the
Tintern woodlands, which were purchased in 1902, serve as examples
of long-sustained forest management, and provide a contrast with the
Commission's younger forests in other parts of the country.

In 1938, all these woods were formed into a Forest Park, to provide
a place of recreation both for those who dwell in their midst and those,
perhaps more numerous, who come on holiday from afar. The passing
years have shown that it is possible to maintain beautiful woodlands,
freely accessible to the public, on the fringe of the busy industrial
communities found in the Dean. Along the Wye Valley it has become
apparent that modern scientific forestry can proceed hand-in-hand
with the preservation of some of our grandest scenery of riverside and
crag, scenery that attracts a constant stream of tourists every summer.
This despite the fact that the needs of the last war led to heavier
fellings than either foresters or lovers of landscape would wish to see;
happily the scars that those exceptional clearances left have now all
been healed by replanting.

Since its creation the Park has been extended by the addition of
St. Pierre's Great Woods near Chepstow, and of several large
woodlands lying to the west of the Wye between Chepstow and
Monmouth. Near Goodrich, the Bishop's Wood has been brought in,
close to Ross certain woods around Penyard Park have been added.
The Flaxley Woods near Blaisdon, and the Clanna Woods not far
from Lydney, are further additions. In these new areas, as elsewhere
in the Park, the same objectives will be pursued, namely the production of timber, combined with the enhancement of the landscape
and provision for its enjoyment by the public. Lovers of our traditional
broad-leaved trees will be glad to hear that much of this new land is
well adapted to the growth of hardwood timbers, which will figure
largely in future plantings.

In the continued use of the camping grounds near Coleford, and
the steady sales of the earlier editions of this Guide, the Forestry
Commissioners have had abundant evidence of the way in which
the Park's facilities are appreciated. It is my pleasant duty, on their
behalf, to extend a welcome to every member of the public, be he
resident or visitor, who comes to share with us the sylvan beauties
of the Dean and its neighbouring woodlands.

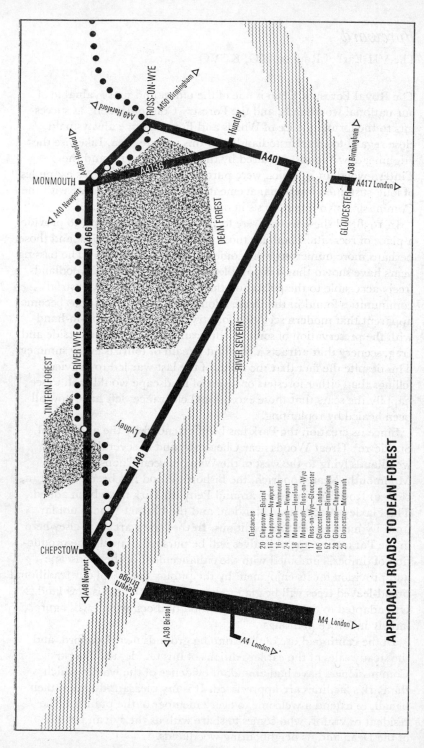

APPROACH ROADS TO DEAN FOREST

ROSS-ON-WYE
M50 Birmingham ▷
A49 Hereford ▷
Huntley
A40
A38 Birmingham ▷
GLOUCESTER
A417 London ▷
A466 Hereford ▷
MONMOUTH
A4136
A40 Newport ▷
DEAN FOREST
A466
RIVER SEVERN
RIVER WYE
TINTERN FOREST
Lydney
A48
Distances
20 Chepstow—Bristol
16 Chepstow—Newport
16 Chepstow—Monmouth
24 Monmouth—Newport
18 Monmouth—Hereford
11 Monmouth—Ross-on-Wye
17 Ross-on-Wye—Gloucester
105 Gloucester—London
52 Gloucester—Birmingham
28 Gloucester—Chepstow
25 Gloucester—Monmouth
CHEPSTOW
A48 Newport ▷
Severn Bridge
A38 Bristol ▷
M4 London ▷
A4 London ▷

Introduction

Can I forget the sweet days that have been
Ere poetry first began to warm my blood
When from the hills of Gwent I saw the earth
Burned into two by Severn's silver flood?
W. H. Davies

In 1924 the Forest of Dean, one of the few survivors of the ancient Royal Forests of England, was entrusted to the care of the Forestry Commission, which has since been actively engaged in its maintenance as a national reserve of growing timber. In 1938 the late Lord Robinson, who was then Chairman of the Commissioners, conceived the idea of declaring the Forest a Forest Park, in order to make its attractive countryside more freely accessible to the public. The Dean was the first area in England and Wales to be so dedicated, and the experience of the past thirty-five years has been that productive forestry can proceed hand in hand with the preservation of the landscape and its enjoyment by thousands of visitors each year.

The Dean is one of the most fascinating regions of England, for its isolation by two great tidal rivers, the Severn and the Wye, and by the hilly nature of its terrain, have preserved a pattern of life and land use different from those found in the rest of Gloucestershire or in the neighbouring counties of Hereford and Monmouth. It is a countryside of small farms and orchards, interspersed with woodlands and commons still browsed by sheep and occasional geese, and diversified by small coal mines and by quarries for sandstone, limestone, and metallic ores. Its heights command some of the finest views in the country, north to the Malvern Hills and the great plain of the Severn, south and east to the rampart of the Cotswold escarpment lying beyond the Severn Sea, and west to the far Black Mountains of South Wales. In contrast, its sheltered valleys are a world on their own, where the visitor may roam for hours amid the tall trees and disturb only an occasional nuthatch or woodmouse. Within a mile or so of some small town or busy highway, he may find that sylvan seclusion that the great woods alone can provide.

Included in the Forest Park are some of the most beautiful stretches of the Wye Valley woodlands, from Hereford and Ross down to Tintern and Chepstow. These include the famous viewpoints around Symond's Yat, Lord's Wood on the Herefordshire bank, and the Highmeadow woodlands around Staunton. Further south the Tintern Forest in Monmouthshire, and the Tidenham Chase woods on the Gloucestershire side, embower the steep and rocky gorge of the river as it winds past Tintern Abbey to meet the tide and the Severn Sea. A little to the west, other woodlands of Tintern Forest stretch across the unspoilt hills of this rural portion of Monmouthshire. The total area embraced by the Park's forests is now 36,500 acres, or roughly 57 square miles.

The extent of the Forest Park is shown on the maps in our centre pages. Details of approaches will be found in the chapter on General Information, which also describes the public camp site near Coleford, which has attracted a constant stream of lovers of the outdoor life since it was first opened in 1939. The rest of the guide consists of chapters on specific aspects of the Dean and the Wye Valley, each by an acknowledged expert who knows the country intimately; and to these authors, as well as to the photographers and artists who have illustrated the text so ably, the thanks of the Forestry Commissioners are due.

Fire brooms

The Forest of Dean - Forest Park

R.G.Sanzen-Baker

The forest 'image'

The name 'Forest of Dean' has a romantic sound and conjures up
countless images, some serene and peaceful, some stirring, others
depressing, but the 'new look' is stimulating and full of possibilities.
The actual survival from prehistoric times of a relatively large area of
predominantly wooded terrain in an otherwise intensively developed
countryside is due to a combination of physiographical, geographical,
and economic factors. The countryside is hilly, even rugged in places.
The soil is relatively fertile, the underlying rocks being Coal Measures,
Carboniferous limestone, and Old Red sandstone. The proximity of
the rivers Severn and Wye has had an isolating effect on the region
and the inhabitants, but the rivers have also provided a contrary
function by supplying the means of transport both for invaders and
exports of iron and timber.

Medieval hunting forest

The Forest of Dean, a hunting-ground of Norman kings, was
certainly used for recreation in those far-off days but only for a
privileged minority and administered under harsh forest laws during
the eleventh, twelfth, and thirteenth centuries, for the protection of
the king's deer and the wild boar. This royal administration involved
numerous officers, most of them unpaid except for perquisites, among
them being the Warden of the Forest, the foresters-of-fee, the
regarders, and the woodwards, but the ancient elected office of
verderer is the only one to survive. There are four of them and they
constitute the Court of Verderers.

The 'Foresters'

The Forest of Dean has been the home of countless generations of
miners and woodcutters. Even in Roman times the miners of the
Forest of Dean attacked mother earth with primitive picks and shovels
to excavate the rich veins of haematite iron ore that occurred in
certain parts of the Carboniferous limestone. The woodcutters and
charcoal-burners supplied the essential charcoal for smelting the iron
in the numerous forges and furnaces.

Extent of the forest

The Forest of Dean, or simply 'The Forest', is regarded by the people
of Gloucestershire as that part of the county lying west of Gloucester
and north of the Severn, with the river Wye forming a boundary to

3

the west and the towns of Newent and Ross-on-Wye lying more or less to the north of the Forest. It is interesting to note that this virtually coincides with the 'statutory' Forest of Norman times. However, by the early fourteenth century many manors in the north, also in the extreme south and south-east of this region, were no longer administered by the king's officers as part of their domain. The boundaries of the present-day 'statutory' Forest, in area approximately 24,000 acres, were defined by perambulation in 1831; the area, in fact, is much the same as it was in Stuart times. Of this area, some 4,000 acres are no longer in the possession of the Crown. The remaining Crown land has been, since 1924, under the management of the Forestry Commission. Numerous acquisitions during the past century and a half have increased the acreage administered, as the Forest of Dean, by the Commission to over 27,000 acres.

Mining

To anyone connected with the coal industry, the Forest of Dean represents a one-time prosperous but now exhausted coalfield, with its stark tips reaching to the sky, its derelict colliery buildings and the inevitable drab miners' dwellings. Fortunately this unattractive image is no longer true, most of the old colliery spoil heaps have been planted up with trees, the buildings either demolished or converted to present-day use as factories, warehouses, or even as a youth centre and an adventure centre: as for the houses, most of them remain but the majority have been modernized and given a 'new look'. But coal-mining has not ceased completely; there are still in operation a few small mines, owned and worked by 'Free Miners', descendants of many generations of Free Miners who are said to have been granted their rights and privileges by the early Plantagenet kings as a reward for services rendered as 'sappers' in various wars and sieges to which they were summoned. These mining rights originally applied to iron ore but eventually covered coal and other minerals; even the quarrying of stone within the Forest is subject to rights and privileges similar to those of the Free Miner. Legally any male person born and abiding in the hundred of St. Briavels, aged 21 years or more, who has worked for a year and a day in a mine, may register as a Free Miner. This does not mean that he can now search for coal at will, but he has the chance of being granted a 'gale' of coal (or iron ore) should one become available (plate 38).

Grazing

The Forest of Dean is one of the few places, possibly the only one of any size in Britain, where free grazing is available to persons who do not of necessity own any land. Nowadays only sheep and to a limited extent pigs are to be seen in the unenclosed parts of the Forest. This

4

is not a question of rights of common but of privilege; the practice has been tolerated for possibly three centuries. But now the wandering sheep are a menace on the roads and in private gardens, the annual cost to the Forestry Commission of fencing against them being at least £10,000. The 'Creed Committee' appointed in 1955 reported to Parliament some two years later with recommendations for dealing with this unrestricted grazing, but as legislation would be necessary no action has as yet been taken. As there is no register of the animals and their owners, only an estimate as to their numbers can be given; the Committee estimated that there were approximately 6,000 ewes and 4,000 lambs in summer with 250 owners or 'sheep badgers' as they are known locally. It is probable that the number of owners is dwindling but there is no evidence of fewer sheep on the roads.

Industrial development
Industrially the Forest of Dean has undergone a peaceful revolution during the past decade or so. As recently as 1955 the principal industry was coal mining, with five major collieries in operation, but within ten years they were all closed down permanently. Other major industrial undertakings that have closed down during the last few years are two iron works, railway wagon repair shops, and an electric cable factory. In spite of fears to the contrary the proportion of unemployed labour has been only slightly above the national average. New industries have appeared, among them two paper mills, a number of light engineering works, a 'pigment dispersal' factory, and a refinery for precious metals, also factories making concrete products and others using rubber, plastics, and shredded wood as their raw materials. A major factor in the redistribution of labour in the area has been the vast expansion of the Rank Xerox plant at Mitcheldean which specializes in the manufacture of photo-copying equipment. There has also been a major revolution in the living standards of the ordinary people, whose status symbol is the motor car. This, together with the great increase in leisure time has created a demand for recreational facilities in the countryside, and where better than in the Forest?

Forest management background
No mention has been made so far of the practice of forestry in the Forest of Dean, nor is it intended to go into detail on this subject. An excellent account of the history of the Forest with particular reference to timber production is given in *Royal Forest* by Cyril E. Hart, M.A., PH.D. (Clarendon Press, 1966). The forester who has not a first-hand knowledge of the Forest of Dean probably has a mental picture of an extensive area of oak high forest, varying in quality from good to poor, interspersed with rough commons overrun by sheep.

5

B

But the forester who knows the Dean and has an eye to 'net discounted revenue' visualizes the magnificent stands of Douglas fir, the high-quality Norway spruce, and robust Corsican pine and regards the area as potentially a highly productive forest, which indeed it is.

For a thousand years, probably considerably more, timber had been in demand to make charcoal for iron-smelting, also in medieval times the forest had to supply timber for mining purposes, oak for ship-building and general construction, and oak bark for tanning. The greatest demand was for small-sized trees, coppice-grown poles, and branchwood from the larger trees. This meant a considerable wastage of timber and of course interfered with regeneration, the process being intensified by the browsing of deer and other animals. The iron forges were closed down by royal decree on a number of occasions to safe-guard the growing stock but such strictures were difficult to enforce.

Exploitation under the Stuarts

It was not until the seventeenth century that any real concern was expressed about oak timber in the Forest of Dean as shipbuilding material, although John Evelyn, writing in 1663, maintained that the commanders of the Spanish Armada in 1588 had been charged with the task of destroying the oak timber in the Dean. The first half of the seventeenth century was a period of tremendous exploitation of the natural forest which was coupled with and largely caused by a considerable expansion of the iron industry and the introduction of blast furnaces with their vast consumption of charcoal. The Stuart kings, James I and Charles I, found in the Dean a ready means of raising funds by the sale of concessions for the exploitation of both timber and iron ore. This culminated in Charles virtually selling to Sir John Wintour of Lydney in 1640 almost the whole of the Forest,

Old-style timber fellers tackling a lodged tree

6

including minerals and ironworks. Fellings went on apace, some 4,000 acres were enclosed for regeneration but the local inhabitants protested violently and petitioned the Crown regarding their loss of rights and privileges. Parliament attempted to restrain Wintour's abuses but in spite of surveys and inquiries little effective action was taken to prevent excessive exploitation as the King was in great need of revenue. Conditions during the Civil War were chaotic; there were exceptional demands for iron from the forges and consequently for charcoal; there was much destruction of property, and timber was needed for repairs. There were also heavy demands for ship-timber, gun stocks, barrel staves, and oak bark for tanning.

Commonwealth conservation efforts

During the Commonwealth regime attempts were made to establish sound management of both the forest and the ironworks. A Commission of 1649 made thorough inquiries and many sound recommendations for the conservation of the forest and regeneration of the devastated woodland, including the expulsion of hundreds of squatters and getting rid of over a thousand goats. Many of the orders of Parliament were not carried out by the local officers and abuses continued. However, in 1653 the Commonwealth Council appointed a Major John Wade as chief administrator; he appears to have established some sort of order, restoring derelict ironworks, building new furnaces, and even creating inclosures for the protection of coppice and young trees. Wade's accounts show that he had acorns and beech-mast collected for sowing in the inclosures and oak and beech seedlings lifted for planting waste ground; thus he was truly a pioneer. Unfortunately, in spite of legal backing, Wade gave up his efforts in 1660, bitterly disillusioned by the violent opposition of the local inhabitants who broke down the inclosures and set fire to the plantations.

Restoration lapse

The Restoration in 1660 saw the appointment of a Commission to take over affairs in the Dean but it also saw there appearance of the old loyalties, particularly the notorious Sir John Wintour who was secretary to the Queen Mother and seems to have impressed Samuel Pepys who described him as 'a man of fine parts'. Pepys, as Secretary to the Navy, wrote that he found the ship-timber from the Dean 'to be exceeding good'—demands for naval timber were now getting quite urgent. John Evelyn also wrote in 1662 'concerning planting of His Majesty's Forest of Dean with oak, now so much exhausted of the choicest ship-timber in the world'. There was now a period of mismanagement and ineffective control. Conflicting interests vied with each other and there was gross exploitation of the resources of the Forest. Wintour continued to enjoy the royal favour and was actually charged with the task of restoring the Forest for the future growth of ship-timber in spite of the fact that he was reported to be employing 500 woodcutters. He was under an obligation to supply considerable quantities of ship-timber to the Navy but in fact only delivered a small part of this. Wintour could not account for the missing timber and was charged for the deficiency. He was discredited. However, his debt to the King was remitted and he was discharged of 'his covenants concerning the improvement of the waste soil in Dean'. Thus ended in 1668 an era of gross exploitation for personal gain; the Forest, apart from the Lea Bailey which extended to about 1,000 acres at the northern tip, was totally depleted of timber-size trees.

The Reafforestation Act of 1668

This year saw the passing of an Act of Parliament that has been regarded as the charter for forest management in the Dean. The Dean Forest (Reafforestation) Act, 1668, authorized the Crown to inclose at any one time 11,000 acres through Inclosure Commissioners. The inclosures were freed of all rights of any description and the number of deer in the Forest had to be limited to 800. Prompt action was taken to appoint suitable officers, including new Verderers. The old court-house at Kensley and the prison in St. Briavels Castle were repaired. The constable-warden, the Marquis of Worcester, and his deputy, Sir Baynham Throckmorton, the two surveyors-general for the Crown lands, and their supervisor, John May, were responsible for carrying out the provisions of the Act. The Treasury kept ordering inquiries and issuing orders, the Navy Commissioners kept a watchful eye on the production of ship-timber with their secretary Samuel Pepys actually inspecting the Forest and committing many of his comments to record. They must have been a very determined body of men to have achieved so much, with relatively little knowledge and experience, and in the face of so much local opposition by people who had been deprived of grazing and other rights and privileges. The King's ironworks in the Forest were still demanding charcoal but in 1674 they were sold for demolition. In the same year Throckmorton was appointed Conservator and Supervisor of Dean. The statutory forest was divided into six walks each under a keeper and six lodges were built each with thirty acres of land attached; the lodges were named after notabilities of the time, one was called after the King and included the courthouse which was subsequently known as the Speech House (plates 5 and 41).

A Royal Commission reported in 1680 that of 23,600 acres more than half were well covered with young oak and beech, many of which were forty years old and over, and other native species. There was still a limited amount of ship-timber in Lea Bailey. The Commissioners recommended the making of more inclosures, the thinning out of the woods where too thick, and the tightening up of supervision together with the better use of the Forest Courts. There was continual pressure to produce revenue from the forest to pay for the administration, for new buildings and the repair of old ones in the Dean, and indeed to raise money for use elsewhere.

In spite of these promising beginnings the history of forest management during the following 120 years is a sorry story. Troubles with the commoners and miners continued, keepers' lodges, pounds, and fences were pulled down, and more often than not repairs were not carried out for years; oak trees were stripped of bark, timber was cut and stolen. Royal Commissions and surveys followed one another in a monotonous succession; Supervisors for the Forest were succeeded by Deputy Surveyors (the first deputy to the Surveyor-General was appointed in 1633). They had a difficult job with the staff at their disposal and poor communications. Some were zealous in the performance of their duties but neither they nor their subordinates were well paid and they had to depend on perquisites; it is not surprising then that corrupt practices were suspected now and then.

During the latter part of the eighteenth century, and reaching a peak during the Napoleonic Wars, fellings in the Dean were on an enormous scale and, despite all the abuses of the forest that had been permitted, large quantities of essential ship-timber were shipped from the Severn-side ports to the principal naval dockyards such as Plymouth and Portsmouth, and even as far away as Woolwich and Deptford. Some building of smaller ships was carried on at local shipyards and timber not required by the Navy, together with cordwood and bark, was sold locally, frequently by auction.

Once again little was being done to encourage and protect regeneration. A Royal Commission of 1788 reported in detail on the administration of the Forest and drew attention to the abuses and dubious practices that were prevalent. Surveyors were employed to assess the growing stock and prepare long-term estimates of expenditure and income. Excellent recommendations were made but little or no action was taken, except there were some changes in administration, some improvements were carried out on the road system in the Forest, and, perhaps most important, more stringent action was taken against those who committed abuses against the Forest.

Nineteenth-century conservation

As the war progressed the need for ship-timber became more urgent; Nelson himself visited the Forest of Dean in 1803 and said that it contained 23,000 acres of 'the finest land in the kingdom' but that it was in a deplorable state. He was very critical of the forest management and blamed the sheep, pigs, and deer for the lack of regeneration.

9

He pointed out many of the abuses being practised against the trees and lack of preventive action. He said that the first necessity was the sowing of acorns in fields and recommended the appointment of new officers of the Crown 'who understand the planting, thinning, and management of timber trees; their places should be so comfortable, that the fear of being turned out should be a great object of terror, and, of course, an inducement for them to exert themselves in their different stations'.

By coincidence in 1803 two new Crown appointments were made: that of Lord Glenbervie as Surveyor-General of woods and forests and that of James Davies as Deputy-Surveyor, Dean. Glenbervie not only made a study of silvicultural practices and applied them in the royal forests but was also responsible for the introduction of conifers as forest trees in considerable quantity. Davies, who was a local land-owner, was assisted by his son Edward who in turn became Deputy-Surveyor in 1808 and subsequently changed his name to Machen. He took up residence at Whitemead Park, the lease of which had been given up the year before by the Earl of Berkeley who was Constable of St. Briavels and Warden of the Forest. Thus Whitemead Park became the centre of forest administration for the Dean and was to remain so for the next 160 years.

Encouraged by Glenbervie, Machen faced his task and much local opposition with determination and vigour. Two professional surveyors, Abraham and William Driver, were given a contract to inclose, drain, and plant up 10,324 acres, that is to complete the statutory 11,000 acres of inclosed Forest. An experienced forester, William Billington, was appointed by the Crown to supervise the work which was completed in 1818. Considerable details of the operations were recorded by Machen, Billington, and the Commissioners of Woods. Oak was the principal species used, both by direct sowing and by plants raised in nurseries, enormous quantities of acorns were imported into the Forest, and it is evident that most of this seed was from Pedunculate oak whereas the native species in the Dean and Wye valley area was the Durmast (Sessile) oak, a view held by Dr. E. W. Jones of the Commonwealth Forestry Institute, Oxford. Of course there was a considerable amount of natural regeneration and coppice growth from the previous crop. Other species used, where more suitable for the site, were sweet chestnut, ash, sycamore, European larch, Scots pine, and Norway spruce.

An important addition to the Crown estate was made in 1817 by the repurchase from Viscount Gage of the High Meadow Estate which contained over 3,000 acres of woodland in the Wye Valley. Machen restocked these woods and carried on with his silvicultural work in the Dean, even planting outside the enclosures large standard trees grown in nurseries. To Machen is due the credit for truly reafforesting the Forest of Dean and giving it the appearance that is now regarded as 'traditional'.

Machen remained in office for forty-six years, that is until 1854. The policy advocated by Nelson of thinning the oaks heavily was carried out to promote wide-spreading crowns suitable for ship-timber; also there was an insatiable demand for bark for tanning and small wood for mining-timber and charcoal. Coal-mining was now getting into full swing although coke had replaced charcoal for iron-smelting. A network of tramways and railroads, at first horse-drawn, that became such a feature in the Dean was being developed. In order to curb abuses and keep a check on timber being removed from the Forest the Deputy-Surveyor was made an Inspector of Railways and each holder of the office up to the present time has held a warrant to this effect; latterly the job has been unpaid!

Machen's regime was not, however, without troubles. In 1831 there were serious riots protesting against the continued inclosure of so much woodland; it is said that about 2,000 inhabitants were involved in pulling down the inclosure boundaries and driving in sheep and cattle. Soldiers had to be brought in to restore order, the culprits had to repair the fences and drive out the animals, while the ring-leader was sentenced to transportation for life.

Some inclosures where the trees were past danger from sheep and cattle were 'thrown open' and between two and three thousand acres of new inclosures were made. By 1848 there were approximately 14,000 acres of plantations, excluding High Meadow, described by an independent surveyor as in general being extremely fine. By the Deer Removal Act of 1850 fallow deer, of which it is thought there were between four and five hundred, had to be officially removed from the Forest. The main object was to eliminate the trouble caused by poachers. Some deer have since returned.

A further factor was beginning to affect forest management by the middle of the nineteenth century—iron was replacing oak for the building of the larger ships and warships; thus the original object for creating or at least replacing the oak forest had disappeared before the crop was anything like mature. It is evident that throughout the most critical period of Britain's naval history the Forest of Dean was the most important and most constant source of shipbuilding timber. The work in the Dean had virtually been of top priority but the reali-zation that this was no longer so did not come suddenly. Naval requirements dwindled gradually, and the Navy purveyor became more particular and more selective in what he accepted.

The close of 1854 saw the appointment of Sir James Campbell, BT., as the new Deputy-Surveyor of Dean and within a few months J. K. Howard was appointed Commissioner of Woods and Forests and together they tried to formulate a new policy for forest management.

The scale of new plantings was much reduced but the thinning of the oak was to continue, although less heavily, in order to provide revenue to meet costs. The deep-crowned trees gradually closed up and the heavy branches became suppressed and liable to infection by the fungus *Stereum spadiceum* which ultimately causes butt rot and depreciates the value of the timber. While there were markets for oak bark and hardwood mining-timber, the steadily increasing imports of both hardwoods and softwoods reduced the demand for home-grown oak. The general effect of these trends was the gradual onset of slackness in the local supervision which tolerated abuses by the ever-increasing local population. Encroachments on the forest increased and the failure or inability to maintain the inclosure fences led to invasion by grazing animals, particularly sheep.

Planned management of the twentieth century
Such was the state of affairs when Campbell retired in 1893 and he was succeeded by Philip Baylis who was a barrister by profession. He quickly assessed the situation with which he was faced and was determined to re-establish the Crown's rights and put a stop to abuses. He was the first Deputy-Surveyor to appreciate the need for forest management according to an approved plan. The then Commissioner for Woods and Forests, E. Stafford Howard, approved of Baylis and his actions and intentions. A breeze of silvicultural revival was blowing through the Forest. A conservator of the Indian Forest Service, H. C. Hill, was commissioned to prepare reports with recommendations for both Dean and High Meadow.

In the early summer of 1897 Hill made his survey of the woods and in the extraordinarily short time of just over ten weeks submitted his report and proposals which were to be the basis of forest management policy for more than a decade. Briefly he was shocked by the open state of the woods and the inadequate ground cover which permitted rank weed growth of bracken, bramble, and grass. Most of the trees were short-boled and heavily branched, the conifers and underwood had been largely removed in the thinnings. He approved of the Deputy-Surveyor's plans to re-inclose woods up to the permitted limit, the replacement of poor crops with conifers, and the re-establishment of forest nurseries. He advocated the underplanting and enrichment of the oak with beech and the planting of oak with larch nurses.

Baylis tackled the work energetically; the 'new look' was unpopular with the sheep owners, and in fact Baylis was proposing to have sheep banned from the Forest altogether when regrettably he died of a heart attack in 1906.

He was succeeded by V. T. Leese who more or less carried on with the existing programme, gradually placing more emphasis on the planting of conifers, particularly Douglas fir, but Norway spruce,

European larch, Scots pine, and even Corsican pine were being planted more extensively. Eventually Leese had a plan to replace 75 per cent of the oak in the Dean with conifers but he was hindered by the difficulty of marketing the oak. The wood distillation works at Cannop were established in 1913 and proved to be a useful outlet for hardwood cordwood and in the subsequent world war a valuable source of charcoal and other by-products. They closed in 1971.

The next Deputy-Surveyor was L. S. Osmaston; he was the first to be a fully qualified professional forester. He displayed little sentimental attachment for the traditional aspect of the Forest and planted conifers wherever possible and now many of his plantations are conspicuous features of the Forest. The 1914–18 war created an enormous demand for timber, particularly softwoods of which there were relatively little, mining-timber and charcoal. The emergency upset the orderly procedure and set up a programme of replacing the poorest oak with conifers as prescribed in his plan prepared in 1915.

After the 1914–1918 war Osmaston and C. O. Hanson prepared a much more stereotyped working plan with compartments and sub-compartments. Oak was to be retained on the most suitable sites, about 25 per cent of the total area, to produce a sustained yield of large timber while the remainder of the woodland was to be maintained as, or converted to, coniferous high forest. Meanwhile the Forestry Commission had been set up and was acquiring considerable areas of ground suitable for conifers. In 1924 the Dean and associated Crown woodlands were transferred to the Commission, in the following year Osmaston was transferred to the New Forest and D. W. Young appointed Deputy-Surveyor for Dean. As a matter of national policy it was decided that the Commission should grow oak and other broadleaved trees on sites deemed suitable. Young prepared another working plan and put this policy into effect, he also recommended the practice of underplanting and enriching crops with beech. Thus the traditional character of most of the Forest of Dean was saved for at least another generation. It is worth noting that at that time amenity was not the main consideration; the broad-leaved policy was intended to provide a reserve of hardwood timber as well as the maintenance of a sustained yield as far as possible.

Young was transferred to the New Forest in 1931 and was followed in the Dean by a succession of relatively short-term Deputy-Surveyors —in fact there were eight, the majority being eminent foresters, covering a period of 23 years. Throughout this period the same general policy regarding the planting of broad-leaved species on suitable sites was followed. There were, however, two events of profoundly different character that were to have a great effect on forest management in the Dean.

In 1938 the Forestry Commissioners announced that the Forest of

Dean and associated woodlands in the lower Wye valley were to be England's first National Forest Park. The outbreak of war in the following year upset plans for development in this direction, but nevertheless a camping ground with pavilion and lavatories was opened in 1939.

In the autumn of 1939 emergency plans were put into effect, placing the Dean on a war-time footing; wood cutters went into action in force under the Home Timber Production Department. The research, education, and publications sections of the Forestry Commission were evacuated from London to Whitemead Park and the Chief Research Officer, W. H. Guillebaud, became, also, Deputy-Surveyor for the Dean. The war created an insatiable demand for pit-props, mining-timber, railway sleepers, and timber for defence works and other purposes; even rather poor quality hardwoods found a ready market. Some 6,000 acres were cleared during the war and the immediate post-war period but even under the stress of the emergency considerable attention was given to the questions of amenity and shelter for the subsequent crop; broad belts of the existing high forest were left alongside many of the roads and across hill-sides. It is due to this act of conservation that the Forest owes much of its 'traditional' appearance at the present time.

Another factor which helps considerably to perpetuate this image of the Forest of Dean is the fact that most of these war-time fellings were replanted with oak and other broad-leaved species, occasionally in mixture with conifers. For almost a decade the emphasis in forest management was on conservation of existing timber stocks, coupled with the rehabilitation of devastated woodland and the afforestation of suitable bare land. There were two conflicting factors to the conservation policy; one was that much of what was left of the old broad-leaved woodland was uneconomic in character, however desirable it might be aesthetically. The other factor that influenced policy was that during the war a considerable number of small sawmills had been established in and around the Dean. They were organized to convert, mostly for mining purposes, the type of timber available, for which there was obviously a fair amount of competition. Here was a market outlet that once lost would be unlikely to re-open, particularly as the mining industry was showing the red light in respect of its ability to continue economic working in many older collieries, including the five major collieries in the Forest of Dean.

A change in national forest policy in 1958 removed the emphasis from conservation of timber stocks to the production of timber as an economic crop. At this time the Dean Working Plan (1949–58) was being revised and consequently the new working plan (1959–68) was based on this policy. Due regard would be paid, of course, to other considerations, such as amenity, recreation, local markets, and other factors. The economic experts demonstrated that Douglas fir, for example, grown on suitable sites to an optimum size could be extremely profitable, other conifers such as Norway spruce and Corsican pine could also be grown profitably; on the other hand broadleaved trees, more especially oak, could not be grown at a profit even on the best sites. Even European larch which had been so widely planted and which grew so well in the Dean could only be grown at a financial loss. The anticipated loss could be made less severe by mixing in some of the money-spinning conifers (plates 1, 13 and 40).

A forest 75 per cent evergreen and 25 per cent deciduous was now envisaged, careful landscaping in the gradual replacement of the existing crops was essential and could create an attractive yet economically viable forest park. The guidance of an eminent landscape architect, Dame Sylvia Crowe, was sought and the principles then put forward are being applied. Beech, which is native to the Forest and grows vigorously, is replacing oak for it is potentially more profitable to grow.

During the next decade fellings of the old oak woods were speeded up to a degree commensurate with the ability of the local markets to absorb the timber and at the same time to maintain prices at a reasonable level. As and when financial and other factors permitted, enrichment with Douglas fir and other suitable conifers was carried out in the post-war plantations of oak, larch and oak, and pure European larch.

As time went on it became clear that in order to safeguard the amenities alongside the highways and elsewhere, also recreational facilities, an amenity 'working circle' was desirable. Plans were prepared covering some 5,000 acres and have now been incorporated in the new working plan (1969–78).

It is interesting to note a change of heart with regard to the post-war oak plantations; it has been decided to allow them to carry on to maturity rather than carry out the costly task of converting them to conifers. Thus the efforts of those who planted them will not have been in vain and the 'traditional' character of the Forest will be retained in part at least for almost another century.

This somewhat lengthy account, although in outline only, could be headed 'the rise and decline of oak in the Forest of Dean' but the end of the story is yet to be told.

Tidenham Chase is now included in the Dean working plan. The total area of the statutory Forest plus areas acquired or leased, less disposals, is 31,382 acres (12,700 hectares); of this some 4,362 acres (1,765 hectares) cover private freeholds and 'waste of the forest' within the statutory Forest. Thus the working plan area is 27,020 acres (10,935 hectares). The table overleaf shows a summary classification of this area.

Recreation and amenity

Prior to 1938 little or no thought had been given to the provision of recreational facilities for the visitor to the Forest of Dean. In fact, apart from Scout troops requiring camp sites more especially in the Wye Valley, there had been no demand for such facilities; the Forest of Dean was not known to the public generally throughout the country.

The fact that there was a substantial area of oak woodland, mostly mature and uninclosed, meant that the amenity issue had not arisen and there was ample provision for the few ramblers and picnickers who ventured into the Forest which was still virtually an industrial area with innumerable pit tips and other ugly scars.

For many years the Crown had shown a sympathetic attitude to the requirements of the local inhabitants for recreational facilities; practically every village and hamlet has its playing field and childrens' playground carved out of the forest at a nominal rent.

Having regard to the amenities of the Forest the 1967 Working Plan prescribed an Amenity Working Circle of just over 5,000 acres; this was increased in 1969 to 7,000 acres. After further consideration of the amenities and landscaping of the Forest it was decided to maintain the status quo which is as follows:

10,000 acres of	Conifer Plantations
6,000	Broadleaved Tree Plantations
7,000	Mixed Conifer and Broadleaved
23,000	Plantation Total
1,000	Scrub (mainly on rocky outcrops—Wye Valley etc)
1,000	Bare or Felled land (plantable)
2,000	Open Forest (Waste land, Water, Highways etc)
27,000	Total Extent of Dean Forest

The annual output from thinnings and clear fellings in the Forest amounted, in 1972, to 22,000 tons of coniferous timber and 15,000 tons of hardwoods cut from broadleaved trees, totalling 37,000 tons in all.

In 1938 the Forest of Dean and neighbouring woodlands owned by the Forestry Commission in the Lower Wye Valley were declared by the Commission as England's first National Forest Park. (Subsequently the word 'National' was dropped to avoid confusion with National Parks promoted by the Countryside Commission.) The total area now covered by the Forest Park is 36,500 acres or 14,500 hectares. The first development was the provision of a camping-ground with a pavilion and toilet facilities at Christchurch near the well-known

Wye Valley viewpoint—Symonds Yat Rock. Any further developments that might have been contemplated were curtailed by the outbreak of the Second World War in the following year.

Considerable areas of woodland were felled during the war and immediate post-war years; generally speaking the impact of these fellings was lessened by the retention of wide belts of standing timber alongside the main roads and in other strategic places. Subsequent replanting was largely with oak and other broad-leaved trees, sometimes in mixture with conifers.

The call of the countryside

Not least among the changes that have taken place during the past two decades is the increased mobility of the general public due to the popularity of the motor car. This has been coupled with a vast increase in the amount of leisure time—longer holidays and long week-ends. The cost of hotel and other accommodation has risen relatively steeply; in fact the demand would probably have outstripped the supply were it not for the growing popularity of camping and caravanning. Other factors have led to an increased interest in the countryside, not only as a sanctuary from the noise and bustle of the town, but as a place to explore and satisfy curiosity, also as a boundless field for recreational activities of the individualistic type such as rambling, climbing, canoeing, caving, and the newer competitive sport of orienteering. Educational developments and broadcasting have stimulated a dormant interest in wild life and conservation. Schools and youth clubs now include camping, hiking, and expeditions in their curricula. Such activities are an integral part of the Duke of Edinburgh's Award Scheme which has given great impetus to the demand for recreation of an adventurous nature for which the Dean Forest Park provides ideal terrain.

His Royal Highness the Duke of Edinburgh stated in 1963: 'We are on the threshold of the age of leisure, and the problem is no longer academic. There are stark and immediate problems facing us. The queues for playing-fields are getting longer; the pressure on general sports and recreation clubs of all sorts is increasing. Swimming pools and sailing clubs are getting crowded, and recreational users of water are beginning to run into each other. . . .It is no longer a question of encouraging people to take part; from now on we have to concentrate on providing facilities of the right sort and in the right place, and properly organized.'

The Countryside Act of 1968 established the Countryside Commission, which incorporated and extended the functions of the former National Parks Commission to conserve and enhance the natural beauty and amenity of the countryside and encourage the provision and improvement of facilities there for everyone's enjoyment. The Act gives powers to local authorities to provide and manage Country Parks which would cater for a wide variety of recreational activities. The Forestry Commission is also empowered to provide facilities for recreation and to improve the amenities where necessary for the enjoyment of the public.

During the past fifteen years the demands of the public for camping and picnicking facilities in the Forest of Dean have steadily increased and it has been Forestry Commission policy to anticipate the requirements of the public and, within the slender financial resources available, to keep slightly ahead of the demand. The Creed Committee in its *Report of the Forest of Dean Committee* 1958 Cmnd. 686, 1959, HMSO, approved this policy and recommended expansion on these lines.

Suitability of the Forest of Dean and Wye Valley

The Forest Park covers an area of approximately 57 square miles on the English-Welsh border, the terrain is hilly, rugged in places. Pedestrian access is virtually unrestricted, the river Wye provides excellent canoeing and fishing, and, with reasonable care, good swimming facilities; sailing is also possible on the Severn. For the rock climbers there are cliffs in the Wye Valley and innumerable quarries, while underground in the limestone areas there are endless caverns and old iron-ore workings for the speleologist to explore.

The Forest of Dean lies immediately north of the A48, Gloucester–Chepstow–South Wales road, and immediately south of the A40, Gloucester–Ross-on-Wye–Monmouth road. Internally the territory is traversed by a network of good roads, three running east–west, the A4135, Gloucester–Longhope–Monmouth, carrying the most traffic, and three running north–south; there are also many good minor roads. At one time the area was covered by an intensive railway system but now no passenger service operates except at the main line station of Lydney.

However, the really significant factors are recent developments: firstly the M5 motorway and the 'Ross Spur', the M50 from Birmingham extending into the reconstructed trunk road, the A40 to Monmouth and South Wales; secondly the Severn Bridge, which is part of the M4 motorway to South Wales, brings the whole of the Bristol area within easy reach of the Forest Park.

It is clear that the Forest of Dean occupies a strategic position as an overnight stopping-place between the north of England and the south-west, also between London and South Wales. There is likely to be an increasing demand for short-stay caravan and camping sites.

Approximate distances and travelling times between the Forest
Park and various centres of population are given below:

Birmingham	70 miles	2 hours	Gloucester	17 miles	½ hour
Bristol	36 miles	1 hour	London	122 miles	3½ hours
Cardiff	46 miles	1½ hours	Swindon	50 miles	1½ hours

The Gloucestershire County Council's survey report, *Outdoor Recreation
and the Gloucestershire Countryside* (published by the County Council in
September 1968), states that the area is within relatively easy reach
of a total urban population of approximately six million people.

Present-day use of the Forest Park

During the summers of 1967 and 1968 attempts were made to assess
the public usage of the Forest Park both by the mechanical counting
of motor vehicles and by interviewing drivers, some of whom agreed to
answer questionnaires. The Geography Department of Bristol
University co-operated with the Forestry Commission in this survey.
This revealed around half a million annual motoring visitors to the
Gloucestershire section of the Forest Park. The majority of these are
day visitors, the average car load being 3·7 persons. The most popular
spots for these visitors are Symonds Yat Rock and the Speech House
area in the centre of the Forest. Of the visitors to Symonds Yat Rock
over 60 per cent come from over 40 miles away, notably the
Birmingham area, while of the visitors to the Speech House woods
over 60 per cent come from 25 miles or nearer. It would appear that
Symonds Yat is better known further afield; it also provides a
magnificent panoramic view. The local people would prefer, it seems,
to have their picnics in the Forest itself. Results of this survey have
since been published as Forestry Commission Bulletin 46, *Forest of Dean:
Day Visitor Survey* by R. J. Colenutt and R. M. Sidaway (HMSO 60p).

The great majority of these visitors want nothing more than to
enjoy the scenery, the out-of-doors, and the peace and tranquillity of
the woodlands. Of course, they need space to park their cars off the
highway and toilet facilities at the more popular places. Some enjoy
walking leisurely through the woods, particularly if their attention is
drawn to points of interest. In 1968 some 20,000 copies of nature trail
booklets were sold and in 1969, Forestry Commission Jubilee Year,
this number rose to 25,000; it should be remembered that a single
copy may represent not merely a family, but possibly a whole class
of schoolchildren or a troop of Scouts; probably five persons per
booklet is a conservative estimate.

It is difficult to give an accurate figure for the number of campers
using the Commission camp sites because of the method of charging.
However, the number of camper/nights, including those in caravans,
at the public camping-grounds of Christchurch and Braceland is

annually about 80,000. The equivalent figure for the youth service sites is estimated at 16,000–18,000.

The Youth Hostels Association state that their hostel user/nights in the locality is of the order of 15,000 annually.

There are also a number of privately owned camping and caravan sites of more recent development which are proving very popular, particularly at bank holiday weekends, because of their cheaper rates of charges, but no information is available regarding the number of campers.

Facilities for recreation (plates 8–10, 18, 19, 22–25, 31–34, 37, 39, 41, 42, 51 and 52)

Public camping and caravanning needs are catered for at the large and well-equipped Forestry Commission camping-ground at Christchurch and its annex half a mile away at Braceland—a former farmstead in the middle of the High Meadow Woods.

There are eight recognized youth service camping-grounds, that is, sites used by schools, Scouts, Girl Guides, and other youth organizations. Three of these sites have toilet accommodation, the others have only the minimum requirements of a water supply, road access, and available firewood in the surrounding woods. The most popular youth service camping-ground is at the Biblins on the banks of the Wye where canoeing and swimming are popular pastimes. Here, also, the river winds its way through the famous Wye Gorge with its limestone crags providing both rock climbing and caving.

The need for all-the-year-round 'camping' facilities led to the provision of 'Youth Adventure Centres' of which there are four. Two are log cabins built by voluntary labour, the Forestry Commission supplying the materials. The first was opened in 1962 at the Buckstone, a well-known look-out point; this has bunk sleeping-berths for twenty persons of one sex. The second is much more ambitious and was opened in 1967 at the Biblins (plate 24). This has accommodation for mixed parties, 18 boys and girls, with separate leaders' rooms. Gloucestershire Education Committee has taken over both of these buildings and has also converted an old farmhouse type of building at Braceland into an adventure centre of similar capacity to that at the Biblins. Bournville College of Further Education has taken over the old office block at the Cannop Colliery site and this has been adapted for use as an adventure centre and field station.

There are three youth hostels in the Forest of Dean area, the major one being at St. Briavels Castle (plate 25), the others at Mitcheldean and Goodrich.

Some thirty miles of 'waymarked paths' have been laid out by the Ramblers' Association in co-operation with the Forestry Commission; these are related to the location of the youth hostels (see page 112).

Symonds Yat Rock has already been mentioned as a focal point for visitors; here the Forestry Commission have provided extensive car parking facilities, a log cabin for refreshments, and a footbridge over the road to the best viewopint. The Rural District Council added a toilet block, built of Western red cedar, and a coach park. The Automobile Association contributed a view indicator on the Rock itself and as a safety precaution the Commission built a parapet wall.

There are some fifteen designated picnic places, the largest and most popular of which is that by the Speech House. Here the Commission have provided two toilet blocks built in Western red cedar, a number of fireplaces and standpipes for water, also a small log cabin for refreshments. The other picnic places, at present, provide much simpler facilities, but they are all in pleasant surroundings and some have extensive views. It is becoming necessary to disperse the visitors to a larger number of sites and it will be almost essential to provide more toilet facilities.

There are some twelve nature trails or forest walks. They vary from short rambles to almost arduous expeditions taking five or six hours to complete or to be tackled in more than one session. They have created tremendous interest and are proving very popular, particularly with the local schools and campers.

The latest attempt to guide the motorist on holiday is the signposting of 'A Scenic Drive through the Dean Forest Park'. There are of course picnic places and viewpoints on the route. A well-illustrated map-cum-information folder is available, price 10 pence. About 3,000 copies were sold during the latter part of the 1972 season.

The public relations side of the Forestry Commission activities in the Forest Park are being handled most ably by a Head Forester who has been designated 'Forest Warden'. The demand for talks and conducted forest walks by schools, Scout camps, training colleges, etc., has been very considerable and is increasing.

Many members of the public have indicated their appreciation of the information services of the Commission locally; these include the erection of signposts, information boards, and the labelling of plantations, forest plots, and individual trees.

Amenity provisions in forestry management

In many Wye Valley woods two methods are employed to avoid the undesirable effects of extensive clear fellings. The major one is the use of group fellings; these groups are five to eight acres in extent. No real problem of management is involved since this size of group provides a good marketable parcel of timber. The groups are replanted immediately, various species, both coniferous and broad-leaved, are used, giving a most pleasing effect on the landscape. The other method is to carry out selective fellings leaving an overwood of the best and most suitable trees for retention and to carry out an 'enrichment' planting using species that are able to stand some shade.

Within the statutory Forest of Dean the restrictions of the inclosure system on forest management necessitate clear fellings generally, but there is one exception, namely in Parkhill near Whitemead Park, where amenity considerations are important: here a 45-year regeneration period is prescribed which involves felling and replanting five one-acre groups each year. Elsewhere in the Forest, screening belts mainly along the roadsides are being retained. During the past decade the practice has been to avoid uniformity by varying the width of the belts, even in places bringing the felling right to the roadside. In strategic positions groups of the old broad-leaved woodland are left, with only selective felling carried out, provided there are sufficient suitable trees to leave standing. Generally speaking replanting is carried out so as to maintain the present balance between broad-leaved trees and conifers. Certain mature avenues and woods of high amenity value are being replaced gradually by group plantings using broad-leaved trees. Variety in the choice of species has had an important effect on the amenity aspect of the Forest generally and latterly special efforts have been made to avoid felling areas of rectangular shape and straight lines on hillsides, but it will be many years before earlier indiscretions can be masked.

The current working-plan for the Forest of Dean, including Tidenham Chase, embodies an amenity working circle of some 7,000 acres (2,266 hectares). This area includes not only roadside woodlands and woods of high amenity value, but open greens where planting is not desirable, reserves for conservational, ecological, and research purposes, picnic places and camping grounds, ponds and quarries, and about 100 acres of farm land.

The intention is to maintain and improve the amenity of the woodlands where seen and frequented by the public, bearing in mind their traditional character and variety of landscape. The existing facilities for recreation and pedestrian access will be maintained and improved whenever possible. Efforts to interest the public, more especially the younger generation, in the work of the Forestry Commission, in the wild life and natural history of the Forest and in conservation will be continued and expanded. These are the functions of a Forest Park.

The future

The arrival of a people possessed of greater leisure, greater mobility, greater freedom, and an urge to visit the wide open spaces is inevitable. Hazards lie ahead and forward planning is the only way of avoiding chaos.

The writer has long maintained that in the not too distant future

the importance of the Forest of Dean as a Forest Park and place of
recreation will far exceed that of a commercial forest, though
obviously the two functions must forge ahead together.

When I sit under a green tree
  Silent, and breathing all the while
As easy as a sleeping child
  And smiling with as soft a smile.
Then, as my brains begin to work,
  This is the thought that comes to me:
Were such a peace more often mine,
  I'd live as long as this green tree.

The Tree   W.H.Davies

Acknowledgement
The writer is deeply indebted to Dr. Cyril Hart, M.A., PH.D., for the
tremendous amount of research he has put into the production of his
various historical books on the Forest of Dean, from which much of
the information in the present article has been gleaned.

The History of Dean Forest

The Rev. Canon R. J. Mansfield

The Severn, Britain's longest river, sweeps from its source in the mountains of Mid-Wales to meet the ocean in an estuary where it is joined by the Wye, which has come from a source on the same mountain by a shorter route. The two rivers enclose much that is lovely in Western Britain, and between them, almost at their point of junction, lies the Forest of Dean, occupying part of a plateau which rises from the Severnside and descends into the Vale of Usk. With the two rivers as its boundary the Dean is practically an island: 'The Eye between the Severn and the Wye'.

It is the insularity of the Forest which has contributed much towards its history. Cut off from both England and Wales by its natural boundaries, and from each other by the rugged nature of its surface, the people of the Dean have developed a sturdy independence over the centuries which is only now softening by the influence of modern communication.

The Dean is old. Its geological strata were laid down many ages ago to form the raw material of an industry which lasted for two thousand years, and with the timber which grows within its bounds these have contributed in no little measure to the story of a unique part of Britain.

Early days

The earliest inhabitants of the district were cave dwellers who lived high above the Wye. It is estimated that the deepest levels of 'King Arthur's Cave,' and its neighbour 'Merlin's Cave,' represent an occupation of twelve thousand years ago when the last Ice Age was receding. The caves were first examined in 1871 and a systematic excavation was undertaken during 1924/27 proving that the cave and its surroundings were occupied by man at least down to Roman times.

Indications that folk of later cultures knew and used the Forest, even if they did not come to live in it, arise from a number of artefacts which have been discovered in the district. Later still megaliths were erected, three of which still survive in the Long Stone, beside the Coleford/Staunton road (plate 12), the Queen Stone at Huntsham and the Broad Stone at Stroat. Other stones are known to have existed but these have been destroyed in more recent days.

It was when the presence of mineral ores was discovered and their use was recognised that man came to live in the Forest and his hill forts or 'burys' survive in place names and in some cases on the ground. Examples in varying states may be seen at English Bicknor,

Soudley, Stowe and Welshbury, while later promontory camps are at
Symonds Yat, with its five banks, Lydney Park and Lancaut. There
are no long barrows in the Dean since the country was not suitable
for the farming population which built them in New Stone Age
times, but a round barrow has been excavated on Tidenham Chase
where other relics of former inhabitants have been found.

The iron ore occurs deep under the Dean but it outcrops round the
Forest in the shape of an irregular horseshoe where for centuries it
was mined by means of shallow workings among the rocks known as
'scowle holes'. Long deserted, many of these have now become
picturesque forest dells and the finest of them is The Bream Scowles,
locally known as 'The Devil's Chapel' (plate 49).

Roman times

The Romans soon discovered the value of the Forest mines and
before long they had established an iron making centre at Ariconium,
a town which has now disappeared but which stood near the present
village of Weston-under-Penyard not far from Ross-on-Wye. A
Celtic tribe had long been settled in a promontory camp above the
valley in what is now Lydney Park, the home of Viscount Bledisloe.
These people had long practised the art of iron working and they
seem to have been left very much to themselves until late in the
occupation when the powers of their local god, Nodens, became
sufficiently well known to warrant the erection of a Temple on the
site in about 367 A.D. The building was novel, displaying charac-
teristics which were later developed in Christian churches rather
than pagan temples. In the same neighbourhood near Woolaston a
large villa with twenty rooms in the main building, as well as several
smaller outbuildings, was discovered in 1934. A few years ago, on

Lancaut Old Church

25

the plain below the temple site, extensive traces of what appears to have been commercial buildings were discovered at Park Farm, close to a dried-up creek which would have given access to the tideway.

During Roman times a road was made from the Lydney district across the Forest for transporting ore to Ariconium. This is 'The Dean Road' a short stretch of which is now kept exposed at Blackpool Bridge showing how the road originally crossed the stream by means of a ford, but was later diverted over the bridge which probably retains at least a few Roman stones after many reconstructions (plate 11).

Several of the roads in the Dean are based upon Roman foundations or upon earlier roads made up to Roman standards, while potsherds of high quality and numerous hoards of coin have come to light in several places.

The Dark Ages

For many years after the Romans left Britain the Forest reverted to Celtic customs, if indeed they had ever been superseded, for the Dean lay just within the "occupied" part of the country rather than the "settled" part as did the Cotswold country.

The Battle of Dyrham in 588 brought what is now Gloucestershire east of the Severn into English hands, but it was not long before they brought the Dean under their rule. English settlement was not possible to any extent until Offa the Mighty built his Dyke "from the Dee to the Wye" and parts of that well-known earthwork may still be seen between Redbrook and Tutshill. But once settled the English soon took control and most of the place names in the district are of English origin. There are several '-tons' usually named after the original settlers, and a good many '-leys' the latter signifying a clearing in the woodland.

During the very disturbed period of Viking raids the Forest suffered together with other parts of the country, its openness to attack from the sea making it especially vulnerable, though there is little trace of the invaders who left no permanent mark. On the Beachley peninsula Buttinton Tump marks the spot where a retreating Danish army held out until it was driven away by Ethelred, the son-in-law of Alfred the Great. English settlements were made along the banks of the two rivers but the central highlands were still unpeopled except for the beasts of the chase, for the Forest had become a hunting ground for the king and his friends by the days of King Canute the Dane.

When boundaries came to be defined the Forest covered a large area. It was not all woodland for a 'forest' was an accepted term for a tract of land which was subject to 'Forest Law'. Its widest bounds were: 'Between Chepstowe Bridge and Gloucester Bridge, the halfe deal of Newent, Ross Ash, Monmouth Bridge, and soe farr into the

Seassoames as the blast of a horne or the voice of a man may be heard'.

The latter definition might imply that boats on the Severn were regarded as being under the jurisdiction of Forest officers as long as they were within hail. Roughly, the rivers Severn, Wye and Leadon were the limits. But as the years went by much of this was deforested, leaving the Dean at about its present dimensions by the middle of the Thirteenth century.

The Middle Ages

The Norman Conquest made little change in the Dean except that English lords were replaced by Normans in the ring of villages which surrounded 'The King's Hunting Ground in Gloucestershire'. Royal visits were not infrequent since it had long been the custom for the monarch and his court to spend the Christmas season in Gloucester. Indeed the manor of Awre was charged with the supply of 'half a night's ferm' probably for those occasions.

The royal chase was first of all in the care of the lord of the manor of Dene who held his land 'free of gheld for guarding the King's forest.' But very soon the district was divided into ten bailiwicks each with its own appropriate officials under the Lord Warden of the Forest and Constable of the castle of St. Briavels, whose headquarters were in that village, which gave its name to the 'Hundred'.

The older churches (plates 27, 29, 30)

The Domesday Survey tells us little about the Forest itself. The survey was made for the purpose of taxation so that the royal chase was not included. Information is given about the ring of manors on the outskirts and although in general religious buildings were not included we know from other evidence that each one of these manors had a Norman church. Norman work survives at Hewelsfield, St. Briavels, Staunton, English Bicknor and Ruardean, with traces in a few other places. Lydney, Awre and Westbury-on-Severn all had churches in pre-Conquest days, but they were rebuilt in the Early English and Decorated periods. There are records of a church standing at Newnham as early as 1018 but its present Victorian church, with a few details of earlier buildings incorporated, was rebuilt after a disastrous fire destroyed a former re-building, completed but six years earlier. The church here has been re-built on two different sites at least five times.

The largest church is that of All Saints Newland. It was built soon after 1200 by Robert of Wakering who made an assart or clearing in the western side of the Forest and founded the village of Wellington which is now called Clearwell. A decision was made very shortly that all new assarts (or clearings for cultivation) in the Dean should be included in the parish of Newland, and so a very large parish resulted which was not divided until well into the nineteenth century. Newland had three chantries, two of which were to have long-lasting effects. The chantry priest of Our Lady's Service was given the obligation of visiting the forges and mine pits 'to say them gospels', and when the chantries were dissolved, chapels of ease rapidly sprang up in the district formerly covered by the chaplain. The priest of the Greyndour chantry had to keep a school which was refounded by Edward Bell in 1580, removed to Coleford in 1875, and which is now combined with East Dean Grammar School in the Royal Forest of Dean Grammar School, bringing with it a tradition of five hundred years.

There was only one monastery in the Forest although the monks of Tintern had certain interests in its Western portion. Milo of Gloucester, Earl of Hereford, a supporter of Queen Maud in her struggle against King Stephen, was killed in a hunting accident in the Vale of Castiard which runs between Mitcheldean and the Severn. His son, in 1140, founded a Cistercian house, on the site of his father's death, at Flaxley, under the invocation of St. Mary de Dene. The Cistercians of Flaxley became engaged in the local iron industry, and felled so much timber that a grant was made to them of 879 acres of woodland for their own use and the name "Abbot's Wood" has survived to this day.

A cell of the Cistercian foundation of Grace Dieu near Monmouth was established for a short time at Stowe near St. Briavels, but the two brethren who occupied it complained of the wildness of the situation and returned to their mother house.

The Free Miners

The primary purpose of the Forest was to provide cover for the beasts of the chase, together with occasional grants of timber for the use of the King's kinsfolk and servants. Richard III granted to his brother, Richard of Cornwall, 145 oaks when he was building Hailes Abbey. But its mineral content, in medieval times, was also regarded as an important contribution to the national economy. Coal was known. There is reason to believe that soot found in the flues of Roman villas in Gloucestershire was deposited by the burning of Forest coal, and coal mining was mentioned at a Justice Seat held in Gloucester in 1282. But it was iron ore that the Dean produced in quantity. The Free Miners, who claimed that their rights has existed 'from time out of mind', had these rights confirmed to them by King Edward I in respect of their skill in undermining the defences of Berwick-on-Tweed during his Scottish wars, to which he took archers and miners from the Dean on several occasions.

The right was granted to any man born of a free father in the Hundred of St. Briavels who had worked for a year and a day in an iron or coal mine within the Hundred, and it gave him the privilege of working with his 'verns' or partners where he pleased, whether on the royal demesne or the lands of private persons. The right was subject to the approval of the Gaveller, the Officer of the Crown who supervised all work in the Dean beneath its surface, and to the payment of 'The King's Penny' which was collected weekly "between Mattins and Masse". The rights were set out in a parchment known as 'The Book of Dennis' and for centuries that book was revered as the foundation of the miners' privileges. These rights, though amended in detail from time to time, still survive and were protected when mining was nationalised.

The iron made from Forest ore was in great demand during the Middle Ages. The smiths in Gloucester obtained a good deal of their raw material from the Forest of Dean and much of it was made into expendable products such as horse-shoes and quarrels for cross bows. The manufacture of quarrels was carried on at St. Briavels by a family named Malemort, and some half a million or so are recorded as having been exported to royal castles for use against the Scots, the Welsh and the French. Even in later days nailyards were common, while pin factories were to be found in several villages. Armaments too were cast in the Dean and in the time of Charles II cannon were cast in the Flaxley valley. Although the premises were turned over to the making of paper in 1682 and have now become a farm house, the name of 'Guns Mills' still attaches itself to the place until this day.

Forest courts

The Vert and the Venison, all growing and living things in the Forest, have always been in the care of the Verderers, four officers "chosen in full county by force of the king's writ" to hold office for life. The office is usually understood to have been instituted in the time of King Canute early in the Eleventh century. They held their Court of Attachment every forty days at Kensley House in the middle of Dean, and although the house fell into decay during the reign of Charles II and was replaced by 'The King's Lodge', the Court familiarly called 'The Court of Speech' was transferred to the new building which soon became known as the Speech House. The court is still regularly summoned at similar intervals but since much of its work is more easily undertaken by the civil authority, it is usually adjourned immediately and, in practice, meets about four times a year to act in such cases as require its deliberations (plate 5).

In medieval days the Forest was divided for purposes of administration into ten bailiwicks, each with its bailiff or Forester-in-fee with minor officials. The tomb of one such Forester-in-fee, dressed in hunting costume as the King's bow-bearer, may be seen in All Saints Church at Newland (see page 115).

C

The other court was that of the Constable. He presided over the Court of Mine Law where his clerk, the Gaveller and a jury of from twelve to forty-eight miners, according to the seriousness of the case heard the miners' pleas, for none but a true Forester was permitted to address the court. In this court the oath was taken holding a stick of holly though in later times the stick was held across a Bible. The celebrated 'Miner's Brass' in Newland Church depicts the costume of a medieval miner, and it is interesting that a photograph, taken about 1850, shows Forest miners wearing a costume which is almost identical with that shown on the brass.

The changing Forest

A change came over the Forest with the advent of Tudor times. Its importance as a royal chase had completely declined, and the growth of the British Navy magnified its importance as a reserve of timber for the dockyards. The iron industry had consumed a great deal of wood, so to prevent further loss the travelling forges were prohibited. For some time Forest ores were taken to a string of new furnaces stretching the length of the Lower Wye Valley and these continued working into the Nineteenth century. At the time when the Spanish Armada threatened invasion a late mention by John Evelyn the diarist records that Sir Francis Drake and Sir Walter Raleigh both came to live in the Forest for a while to protect the timber, although it is more probable that they came to confer with Sir William Wintour who lived in Lydney and who was Admiral of the White in the Armada action (see plates 16 and 36).

But worse was to come for the Forest under the early Stuarts. In his endeavour to raise money without the consent of Parliament King Charles I granted leases in the Dean for substantial sums to men who exploited the district. The Foresters raised strong objections to this incursion into their privileges, which came to a head when the king sold the Forest to Sir John Wintour for £106,000 to be paid in instalments and a fee-farm rent 'for ever.' In the hope of obtaining quick returns Sir John embarked upon a programme of large enclosures and heavy felling which enraged the natives, turning them away from their traditional support of the king when the Civil War began, and contributing in no small measure to the eventual defeat of the Royalists. The attitude of the Foresters prevented a close investment of Gloucester, whose resistance to the Royalist siege was fatal to the swift advance which would have decided the war in the King's favour.

During the progress of the war a number of small actions took place in the Dean, and Coleford, Westbury, Littledean, Newnham, Highnam and Beachley all saw engagements. A battle at Barber's Bridge which occurred during the siege of Gloucester is commemorated by a roadside cross on the Gloucester to Newent road. The Royalists left the Forest to their opponents who appear to have treated it little better. Such timber as remained was heavily cut by the men of the Protectorate, and though plans were made for re-afforestation, little was done to implement them except for evicting some of the people from about four hundred cabins in the woods where they had fled for refuge. At the same time orders were given for all the iron works to be demolished.

Reconstruction

With the restoration of the monarchy the Dean entered into a new phase of its existence. Though Sir John Wintour revived his claim to ownership he was overruled and a Commission was set up to enquire into the state of the Forest. It was time that something was done since, between Wintour's fellings and wastage by storm—Samuel Pepys reports that in one night a thousand oaks and as many beeches were blown down in one Walk—the Forest was in a poor state, indeed there is at least one contemporary reference to 'the late Forest of Dean'.

Accordingly sweeping changes were introduced. The medieval bailiwicks were abolished and in their place the district was divided into six 'Walks' with a keeper's lodge in each. These were Walks called by the names of the King, his brother the Duke of York, and other distinguished persons of the day, and it was resolved that the Dean should be devoted to raising timber. The Forest people however were still very unsatisfied and a period of unrest and even of rioting ensued. Indeed the Seventeenth century closed with matters in such a state that the Dean at that time was described as 'almost without inhabitants'.

A long period of discussion followed. The Crown sought to improve the yield of timber, and the Court of Mine Law endeavoured to clarify the position of the miners, while at the same time the mining of coal grew steadily, increasing with the general application of power to industry. Before the end of the eighteenth century 121 coal pits were working in the Forest, producing 1,816 tons each week. The pits were small with an average work-force of about half-a-dozen men, but the requirements of industry were such that the Free Miners obtained powers to dispose of their rights to outsiders who were able to provide capital and extend operations, so that by 1832 Edward Protheroe was working thirty-two pits and employing 500 men.

The iron trade too began to improve. Works were opened in the Cannop valley at Parkend and Lydney, and the little river was dammed to provide a head of water to operate a fifty-six-foot water wheel at the Parkend works. Works were installed too in the Cinderford and Soudley district where similar ponds were formed, and the town of Cinderford spread across the hillside, joining a

31

number of small settlements into an urban area.

Obviously with the growth of local industry the workers were not content to live far away from their work, and a number of them employed an illegal, but widespread, practice whereby they believed that by enclosing a plot and building a hearth so that smoke might rise from it overnight without being observed, they gained the right to build a house on that spot. This practice of the "squatters" accounts for the peculiar appearance of many Forest hillsides where the original houses, later increased by in-filling, are scattered with no attempt at planning.

In order to serve the rapidly increasing population and the demands of local trade, tramroads were constructed to cover the district. A main line ran from Lydney to Lydbrook with many branches leading to mines and quarries, while another ran from Bullo, the Severnside port, to the Cinderford district, piercing on its way the Haie Hill with what is reputed to be the earliest railway tunnel in the world.

But the Foresters were still unsettled. The opening up of their district again seemed a threat to their ancient privileges and the year 1831 saw an outburst of riotous destruction aimed against the banks and fences of the enclosures. So in the same year a commission, which sat during the next three years, was appointed to inquire into various matters concerning the Dean.

The Commission of 1831

Among other things it was revealed that the squatters had encroached upon over two thousand acres of Crown lands and all that could be done was to recognise the position and give them their deeds. Among other matters considered by the Commissioners were 'certain claims of common or pasture', for the settlers in the woodland had taken advantage of certain limited rights of "turn out" into the Forest for their animals. Custom had so confused the issue that the Commissioners were unable to come to any decision on this subject, which is still a matter of debate. The rights and privileges of the Free Miners too were studied, but beyond making a few amendments of practices which time had rendered obsolete, these were confirmed in principle.

One of the major issues with which the Commission had to deal was the parochialization of the Dean. The ancient parish of Newland now included several districts with sizeable populations which were situated far from the parish church, and although there were a few chapels-of-ease, especially along the ironstone belt to the West, the newer coal-mining districts were poorly served.

The first church to be built in the nineteenth century was that of Christchurch, Berry Hill, which had come into being by the exertions of the Revd. P. M. Procter, the vicar of Newland, in 1816.

This was quickly followed by the erection of Holy Trinity, Drybrook, as the result of the labours of the Revd. H. Berkin, the vicar of Mitcheldean. A third church, that of St. Paul, Parkend, followed in 1822. But even so, all these, together with the chapels of ease, were not parish churches and the Commission decided that they should all have parishes attached to them and that further parishes should be formed at Cinderford, Lydbrook and Viney Hill. During the course of the century other churches were built in the Forest and parishes were assigned to them, so that we have the present situation that in the outer ring of villages there is a church in each, whose building or tradition goes back at least to the Twelfth century, but within the Forest itself all of the churches are of the Nineteenth.

Meanwhile, in many places individual Free Church ministers had opened places of worship which attracted the support of many of the Foresters, whose independent character had encouraged the growth of Nonconformity.

Prosperity and depression

And now began an era which promised prosperity to the Forest. The clarification of miners' rights provided the means whereby coal mining became a major industry. It was now possible for companies to be formed to sink collieries at least into the middle series of the fourteen or so seams which made up the coalfield and which had been out of reach of the Free Miners. A number of colliery enterprises were

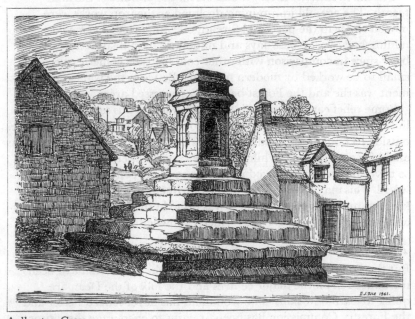

Aylburton Cross

33

started, small at first but attracting more and more capital until by the middle of the century sizeable pits had been sunk in the middle of the coalfield, a large number of men were employed and the Forest gained its reputation as a coal-mining district. More and more large collieries were opened and by the time that the Act of 1904 gave the Gaveller power to re-arrange gales into large areas, the Dean was making a substantial contribution to the nation's coal supply.

Communications too were being improved. The tramroads were converted into railways and all the Forest towns and many villages were linked by rail to the main lines which bordered the district. The Forest's own line, The Severn and Wye Joint Railway, possessed two notable pieces of engineering in its system. One was the viaduct at Lydbrook leading to a junction with the Great Western's Wye Valley line, while the other was The Severn Railway Bridge, opened with ceremony in October 1879 as the first crossing over the river ever to be made below Gloucester, where the two channels of the river had allowed a passage even by Roman times. This bridge remained in service until 1960 when an oil barge brought down two of the smaller spans in fog, after which the bridge was demolished. Now the Forest lines, apart from the main Western Region line from Gloucester through Lydney to Chepstow and Cardiff, have been taken out of service. Their tracks have been removed except for the stretch between Lydney and Parkend which a local Railway Society is hoping to operate as a tourist attraction.

But the twentieth century did not fulfil the promise of the nineteenth. The age-old iron-mining declined as the iron works were moved closer to the ports and foreign ores imported. Even coal mining had seen its best days and nationalisation dealt it a death blow since in comparison with other coal fields its collieries were too small to be worked by modern methods. Between the wars unemployment was rife and the Forest became a depressed area.

Some relief came with the introduction of the bus services which linked every village in the Dean with others and with the larger centres outside its boundaries, and gave opportunity for its people to travel far afield for employment, while the same services opened up the district as never before, and allowed its people to make contact with a larger world. This may have worked to the detriment of the local shopkeepers, much of whose business was done in the evenings at the weekend, when Forest towns were formerly crowded with shoppers.

The Forest of today

But the Forest has weathered the storm. Light industries have been introduced in all the major centres and the folk of the Dean are quick to learn new skills. The woodland has never looked better and the Forestry Commission has been at pains to encourage the visitor to a district which has retained its original wooded character better than any other part of Britain.

Many delightful amenities have been introduced to tone with their surroundings in the shape of picnic areas, timber shelters, kiosks and camping sites with waymarked paths and a scenic drive which makes a complete circuit of some of the most attractive parts of the Forest, including parking sites, picnic places and a number of interesting features.

The Forest is changing. But it has changed many times before. Its old reputation as a coalfield to be avoided has passed away and it is now recognised as a place open to all kinds of people who wish to enjoy its many attractions, and to study the various aspects of a district which is rich material from many points of view.

Its older residents may take a little while to accustom themselves to their guests, but they are rapidly mellowing as newcomers settle among them, and as their own young people make contact with a wider horizon. But pride in his home and the affection he shows even after long absence is still a mark of the old Forester wherever he is to be found, and even if changes continue, the Dean will long remain as the poet Drayton once called her 'The Queen of Forests All'.

Nor wilt thou then forget
That after many wanderings, many years
Of absence, these steep woods and lofty cliffs,
And this green pastoral landscape, were to me,
More dear, both for themselves and for thy sake!

Wordsworth

The Wye Valley and its Woodlands

Herbert L. Edlin

It is to the woodlands that clothe the steep slopes of its gorge that the Wye owes the unique beauty of its lower reaches from Monmouth down to Chepstow. Areas under the care of the Forestry Commission are included in the Park (unless prevented by conditions of tenure) and are indicated on the maps. After half a century of forest management, designed to combine valuable yields of forest products with amenity, the results have proved worthy of inclusion in the Lower Wye Valley Area of Outstanding Natural Beauty—in co-operation with the Countryside Commission, Nature Conservancy and County Authorities concerned.

The Forestry Commission estate is administered on the western (Monmouthshire) side by the South Wales Conservancy from Cardiff and on the eastern (Gloucestershire) side by South West England Conservancy from Bristol with a local office at Coleford. Within the area, local administration is based on forest or section such as those named Tintern, Chepstow, Tidenham Chase and Highmeadow—which are described below, and whose telephone numbers can be found under "Forestry Commission", in alphabetical order in the directories, should you wish to make local enquiries.

The countryside and its history

Below Ross the river Wye, pursuing its southward course to join the Severn, enters a deep gorge which it has cut through the hills, which rise to a height of 1,003 feet at Trellech. From Goodrich, on past Symonds Yat, and towards Monmouth, much of its course lies through Carboniferous Limestone, here cleft by the waters into a picturesque chasm with gleaming white cliffs. Thereafter the underlying rocks are a red sandstone or conglomerate of the Old Red Sandstone series, and the slopes, though often very steep, are not precipitous. But to the south of Tintern village the river runs again through the white rocks of the Limestone, which appear as sheer cliffs at the Wyndcliff and the Piercefield Cliffs in Monmouthshire, and also around the Ban y Gor rocks and Wintour's Leap on the Gloucestershire side. Throughout this tortuous course the Wye runs nearly at sea level, and tides run up it regularly as far as Llandogo, sometimes extending to Redbrook.

Plate 1. Corsican pines

Plate 2. Leafless oak in winter

Plate 3. Beech

Plate 4. Beechwood in spring

Plate 5. The Speech House

Plate 6. Symonds Yat Ferry

Plate 7. Coleford: the square with its clock tower and cross

Plate 8. Holiday centre at Bracelands, near Coleford

Plate 9. Riders

Plate 10. The log-cabin refreshment hut at Symonds Yat

Plate 11. The Roman road at Blackpool Bridge — and an abandoned railway

Plate 12. The Long Stone, a prehistoric landmark beside the Monmouth road, near Staunton

As Tennyson wrote in his *In Memoriam*:

> *There twice a day the Severn fills,*
> *The salt sea-water passes by*
> *And hushes half the babbling Wye,*
> *And makes a silence in the hills.*

Such a remarkable gorge, running through such steep and broken uplands, seems destined by nature to form a political boundary between the territories that it divides; and in fact much of the history of the valley records border wars. Amongst the oldest relics of the past are four bronze axe-heads, unearthed during forestry operations near Liveoaks Farm; similar axes have been found at Tintern, and the three standing stones at Trellech ('Harold's Stones' on the map) also date from the Bronze Age and appear to have been used, like Stonehenge, to follow the course of the sun. In the pre-Roman Iron Age, small defensive camps commanded the crossings of the Wye; traces of these may be seen near Trellech Cross, in the Black Cliff, Wyndcliff, and Piercefield Woods, and also south of Chepstow. The Romans dominated the western bank of the Wye from their walled fortress, still well preserved in outline, at Caerwent (Venta Silurum); their great roads crossed the river at Chepstow and Monmouth, with, perhaps, a link on the west bank through the uplands where the Tintern Woods now stand. The Saxons reached, but did not cross, the Wye; and Offa, King of Mercia in the eighth century, built his famous boundary dyke on the eastern or Gloucestershire side, where it can still be seen at several points between Redbrook and Chepstow.

But it is to the Norman Marcher barons, with their uneasy over-lordship of the ancient Welsh Kingdom of Gwent, that we owe the finest historical monuments in the neighbourhood of Tintern. It was they who built the impressive bulk of Chepstow Castle to guard the southern crossing of the Wye and the Monnow Bridge at Monmouth with its unique arched gateway. Ross Castle is also at a bridgehead, and so is Goodrich Castle, while St. Briavels Castle stands on a hilltop opposite Tintern, to guard other possible crossings against invasion by the Welsh. Further west, the Normans set up castles at Raglan, Usk, and Newport.

It was a Norman lord of Chepstow, Walter Fitzgerald, who in 1131 invited the Cistercian monks to establish their first abbey at Tintern. The later building, whose ruins still stand so magnificently between the winding Wye and the forested hills, was begun in the year 1220, but not completed until the fourteenth century (see cover picture). The Cistercians were active in bringing into cultivation wasteland and forest in wild and undeveloped regions; and this may account for their settlement at Tintern. Here they were, no doubt, amongst the first cultivators of the valley fields and the more fertile hill tops. It is unlikely, however, that the steeper slopes, on which most of the woodlands stand, were ever enclosed for agriculture.

Most of the place names along the lower Wye are of Welsh origin, and a Welsh chieftain named Tewdrig, or Theodorick, King of Glamorgan, is said to have defeated the Saxons hereabouts in the year 600 A.D. He is reputed to have lived at Tintern and its name may be derived from the Welsh *dinas teyrn*, the fort of the king. But in Norman times much of the land was included in the great Forest of Striguil, which took its name from the Welsh name for Chepstow, meaning the bend of the river. Old records still exist of the payment to the Lord of the Manor of Striguil, of curious dues, such as *pannage* for allowing pigs to feed on acorns in the forest. A toll was taken of honey gathered by bees kept in the woods, and another, called *woodehenne*, of all hens. Some tenants paid *woodgavelsilver* instead of delivering firewood to the castle; others could only have brushwood in return for oats supplied to the Chief Forester. Deer were hunted with greyhounds and falconry was practised. In the reign of Edward I there was appointed a "Collector of Money from the sale of wood"; and in the time of Edward III charcoal sales are recorded at Penallt and Trellech.

Owing to its strategic position at the gateway to Wales, Chepstow Castle and the Tintern woodlands were always held by influential families. From the de Clares they passed to the Strongbows, the Marshals, again to the de Clares, then to the Warrennes and the Bigods. In 1468, by an exchange, the lands came into the possession of the Herberts, passing later to the Somersets, Earls of Worcester and later Dukes of Beaufort, who held them until 1902. Then the Tintern woods were sold to the Crown to be transferred eventually to the Forestry Commission between 1924 and 1926. The earlier owners made large gifts of land to the monks of Tintern Abbey, but on the Dissolution of the Monasteries in 1537, these lands came into the possession of the Earl of Worcester. In the sixteenth century Tintern became famous for its wire works, which continued in use until about the year 1900; these derived their power from the waters of the Angidy river, which were made to turn a succession of waterwheels as they descended the valley, where the mill dams are still to be seen. Iron ore was available locally, being found in irregular pockets in the limestone rocks, and the charcoal for smelting came from the woods. Wire for the first Atlantic cable was drawn here.

To the botanist the most interesting features of the Wye Valley woods are perhaps the sharp contrasts afforded by the plant associations of the limestone rocks, the sandstone woodlands, and the moors of peat and heather on the uplands. The waterside vegetation of the Wye and several lesser streams is also of interest. One attractive alien of the brooksides is the golden yellow monkey flower, *Mimulus langsdorfii*. Bird life is rich and varied. Mammals to be found in and around the woods include badgers and the otters which pursue the salmon of the Wye. Deer, strange to say, are still rare, although there are herds of wild fallow deer in the Highmeadow woods and in Monmouth Forest, a few miles to the west; sometimes a stray roe deer is observed. Grey squirrels have become common, despite measures to keep their numbers down.

Tintern Forest

Tintern lies immediately west of the Wye in Monmouthshire. Its 9,500 acres of woodland in the Forest Park region extend from the outskirts of Monmouth South to around Chepstow, and over the 1,000-foot ridge to Trellech, Devauden and Shirenewton, with outliers as far west as Raglan and Llangwm.

The locality has been heavily wooded since ancient times and the forest still clothes the slopes and high ground. Oak and beech are common, and ash, sweet chestnut, sycamore, birch, lime and yew are found on the steep but often sheltered slopes of the Wye and its tributary streams. Coniferous trees were introduced in 1850 and a few magnificent old woods of larch in mixture with beech and oak can still be seen near the Whitestone car park above Llandogo. The deciduous larch and evergreen Douglas fir and pines with some spruce have been extensively planted on the high plateaux areas, and used in the restocking of some felled or derelict woods elsewhere. Discerning visitors will often find that broadleaved woods and groups of oak and other hardwoods have been retained or planted to add variety to the scene.

The steep hanging woods of the Lower Wye Gorge near Chepstow, with its 700-foot limestone cliffs, are of particular interest to forester and naturalist alike. They carry rare remnants of natural growth, and some 200 acres form the Blackcliffe and Wind Cliff Forest Nature Reserve managed by agreement between the Forestry Commission and the Nature Conservancy.

Here the lime tree—uncommon in Britain in the wild state—grows with oak, ash, beech, crab apple, whitebeam and ancient yews. In the underwood spindle, dogwood, guelder rose and hazel are found, and traveller's joy trails in profusion over trees and bushes alike. There are car parks at the Lower and Upper Wind Cliff and a nature trail, set out by the Monmouthshire Naturalists' Trust and the Nature Conservancy, starts from the upper car park.

Driving or walking through Tintern Forest the traveller will find a constantly changing scene from the rolling farm-land and woodland in the south and west, the wooded lower gorge, the softly rounded hills and serenity of the valley near Tintern Abbey, the intimate small side valleys with their cottages, small fields and orchards, nestling in the tall trees, to the coniferous forest and heathland on the ridge and plateaux tops. Here there is indeed much to delight the eye, and here and there places where time seems to have stood still.

The forest is, however, also a place of work and a source of valuable timber products. Some fifty people using the most modern techniques are directly employed by the Forestry Commission, and a further ten work regularly for timber contractors in the area. About 100 acres are planted or replanted every year and the output of timber from thinning and felling currently averages 17,000 tons per year. Many of the traditional markets for small hardwood material are no longer available, but hardwood poles are suitable for the Sudbrook Pulp Mill near Chepstow and good quality turnery poles are still in demand. The smaller coniferous poles are converted mainly into pitwood for the South Wales coalfield and to pulpwood for the board mills at Chepstow or Bristol. A high proportion of the annual output of timber is of sawlog size and here there is a ready outlet in the sawmills in South Wales and South West England for buildings, packing cases and motorway fencing. Some visitors will find much to interest them in the working operations of the forest, but common sense should be exercised to avoid such dangers as falling trees and busy machinery.

The Chepstow section of Tintern Forest may conveniently be reviewed as three groups of woodland. The first of these, Chepstow Park, lies south of the Tintern woods, between Devauden and Glyn, on a great hill of sandstone rising to 932 feet above sea level. The wood formerly carried a rough crop of oak coppice which was cut at intervals for pit-wood and bark. It was replanted with conifers between 1922 and 1950. Chepstow Park Wood is not included in the Forest Park, but its trees are clearly in view from rights of way that neighbour it and the public footpaths that traverse it. There are wide views southwards towards the Severn.

The second substantial group of woods, acquired in 1937, comprises a continuous range on the hills from one to two miles west of Chepstow town, including Fryth Wood, Barnets Wood, and St. Pierre's Great Woods. These have gradually been converted from coppices of oak and birch, unproductive by modern standards, to plantations of beech, oak, larch, and Douglas fir, together with a small area of lime. A delightful approach to them lies along the narrow by-road from Chepstow to the picturesque hamlet of Mounton, with its winding stream, limestone crags, ornamental gardens, and tiny church. In the spring, St. Pierre's Great Woods abound with bluebells, primroses, pale windflowers, and rose-pink campions, and this delectable display has been made more readily accessible through the provision of firm footpaths.

The third group of woods in the Chepstow section consists of more than twenty-five blocks of former coppice and scrub lying in the triangle formed by the three villages of Shirenewton, Llangwm, and Devauden. These are quite recent acquisitions, dating from 1953 on, and they illustrate the problems facing the Forestry Commission in restoring to full productivity the widespread but scattered woodlands of Gwent. Nearly all of them carried only scrub when taken over, and in most places the forester is obliged to grow a first main crop of some vigorous conifer, such as Japanese larch or Douglas fir. Later on, it may be, they will be found suitable for a proportion of hardwood trees, such as oak and beech. (Many of these scattered woods appear on the maps, the others towards Llangwm are omitted through lack of space.)

Tidenham Chase

Although this section of the Dean Forest is wholly in Gloucestershire, much of its 1,961 acres lie so far down the steep sides of the Wye Valley that they are best seen from the Monmouthshire side. In fact the best way to reach them is by the footbridge over the Wye, approached by a path opposite the Royal George Hotel at Tintern. These hillside woods, with their dark masses of yews, broad sweeps of mid-green broadleaved foliage and pale green larches, broken by the white cliffs of limestone, contribute much of the grandest scenery to the Wye between Tintern and Chepstow. Offa's Dyke, an ancient Saxon earthwork, runs through them from north to south, marking the old frontier between England and Wales. Badgers and foxes roam

Wintour's Leap

through them, though the deer that gave the Chase its title are now seldom seen. The birds of the sea wing their way up the course of the tidal Wye, and the rare peregrine falcon has been known to nest on the steeper cliffs. One hidden cleft in the hills, high above the winding Wye, is called, with good reason, the Nightingale's Valley; it is situated about 1½ miles south-east of Tintern as the crow, or the nightingale, flies across the river.

Some of the old woodland that makes up this forest consists of Sweet chestnut, and this is still worked on the traditional plan of 'coppicing', which provides durable fence stakes and posts. The eastern portions, on either side of the Coleford-Chepstow road, are planted in the main with coniferous crops, mainly of larch, for the soil there is poorer, and the exposure more severe; at their highest point the woods of Tidenham Chase stand 700 feet above the Severn Sea. The Devil's Pulpit, a singular pillar of limestone one mile south-east of Tintern, commands a wonderful view of the Abbey, framed in its encircling hills.

High Meadow Woods

The High Meadow Woodlands, most of which were acquired by the Crown from Viscount Gage in 1817 and 1824, form an estate of 3,560 acres around the village of Staunton. Lying in the three counties of Gloucester, Hereford, and Monmouth, they link the Dean forest itself with the woods of the Wye Valley. On the north and west, where they border the river, the rocks are of limestone, which is dramatically exposed in the sheer cliffs of Symonds Yat Rock. From the Christchurch camping ground, that famous view-point is reached by following a waymarked path, or else the public road, due north for two miles; a car park and a refreshment pavilion, built as a log cabin, have been provided as well as toilets. From the cliff top, four grand stretches of the Wye are seen, two on the north forming a sweeping ox-bow around Huntsham Hill, another to the north-east, sweeping below Coppets Hill, and the fourth running down below Lords Wood into the Wye Gorge. The narrow road then descends steeply northwards; by turning left a hundred yards on, following the waymarked path, one may reach Symonds Yat East and cross the threepenny ferry to Symonds Yat West, which is on a bus route. Or by going straight on over Huntsham Bridge, one may gain access to Goodrich, Whitchurch, and Symonds Yat West by road. Pedestrians, however, may prefer to climb down one of the footpaths that lead more directly to Symonds Yat East.

West of the Wye, on Great Doward Hill in Herefordshire, stands the detached portion of Highmeadow known as Lords Wood. A good footpath may be followed from Symonds Yat southwards to view the Wye Rapids and the remarkable Seven Sisters Rocks, while it is possible to follow other tracks north to public roads on Great Doward. The suspension bridge that forms a link with the southern bank of the Wye at the Bibblins, was rebuilt by the Forestry Commission in 1958. Also on the limestone, but on the Monmouthshire side near Reddings Enclosure, is the ecological reserve described in the chapter on plant life.

The rest of the High Meadow property lies on Old Red Sandstone or the Coal Measures, and on the eastern edge of the woods one may occasionally come across the shallow workings of the Free Miners.

The Suckstone, in Reddings Enclosure, interests geologists as being an enormous detached mass of sandstone, estimated to weigh 12,000 tons. The Buckstone, close to Staunton Meend Common, half a mile south-west of Staunton village, will interest the ordinary visitor because of the magnificent views that it commands over both the Wye gorge and the Forest of Dean; it stands 915 feet above sea level. (plate 50). There is a log cabin used as an adventure centre by youth organisations close by.

There are many fine stands of coniferous trees, including sample plots which are measured at intervals as indicators of timber production, but the broadleaved woodlands are even more outstanding. Exceptionally fine oaks occur, as well as limes, yews, and ash trees. Formerly much of the area was managed on the Coppice-with-Standards system, but in recent years the shrubby coppice has been converted where possible to what is called High Forest. Of course, this takes time, but the new stands are not only interesting to the forester but also exceptionally attractive to the eye, as will be realized by anyone who follows the high road between Monmouth and Staunton, or that from Monmouth towards Ross. A herd of fallow deer, survivors of the old Dean stock, still haunts these woodlands.

How many buds in this warm light
Have burst out laughing into leaves!
And shall a day like this be gone
Before I seek the wood that holds
The richest music known?

Wasted Hours   W.H.Davies

The Wild Life of the Dean Region

M. F. Wearing

Throughout the Forest of Dean's history the woodland and wild life has been dependent on the forest environment. As our countryside changes so does the wild life living in it. Some species are lost while others are gained as new and varying habitats are formed. This is true of the changes rung throughout the forest by the foresters. The areas of oak woodland now conserved hold many of the traditional woodland species, while the constant fellings, replantings and tending of the crops until felled again provide a wide variety of varying habitats. This process ensures an equally varying variety of wild life.

Before discussing these situations as they exist today let us look briefly at the Dean's history.

It was the Forest deer that probably ensured the survival of the Forest in the early days, and it's preservation as a Royal hunting area. These original herds of Fallow Deer existed until about 1855 when they were finally eliminated to bring about a cessation of the constant clashes between poachers and the Foresters. Only a few years earlier there had been perhaps 400–500 deer in the forest. Red Deer were briefly introduced in 1842 but only survived a few years, the last being killed in Sallow Valletts in 1848.

Following Nelson's survey of the Forest in 1802, intensive oak plantings were carried out to provide the Navy with timber. It is these plantings that provide much of the older oak woodland that exists today. The first conifers were introduced in the 1780's. Remnants of a group of Weymouth pine, can still be seen near Cannop.

In the modern Forest two Fallow Deer herds exist, while a third enclosed herd is maintained within the confines of Lydney Park. The largest wild herd wander throughout the High Meadow Woods often crossing the Wye into the Doward. These animals are thought to have originated with escapes from Monmouthshire deer parks. A smaller but robust herd exists in the area of the Speech House. These may have come more recently from the now non-existent Courtfield herd, and contain some fine black bucks. As yet the dainty Roe Deer has not arrived, nor the introduced Muntjac, but with the ever-increasing range of these animals in Southern England both could one day become Dean residents.

The animal that has had the greatest affect on the Forest is the Sheep. Their constant grazing on the open forest has created the clean floor effect. Wherever the Forester has enclosed land, the change has

Plate 13. Sunlight and shadow on Soudley's Lower Pond; Douglas firs beyond

Plate 14. The Wye below Symonds Yat viewpoint looking downstream and North towards the Plain of Hereford

Plate 15. The easterly curve of the Wye below Symonds Yat viewpoint, looking upstream – towards English Bicknor

Plate 16. Drake's House at Gatcombe beside the Severn

been dramatic. Shrubs, brambles and many herbs all spring up, providing essential cover for the smaller animals and birds. The harvesting of a forest crop radically alters a woodland habitat, but where economic forestry is practised does not destroy it, for with care, there are always tree crops at varying stages of development.

Felled areas provide an ideal situation for Nightjars, where on a warm summer evening their constant 'churring' may be heard. Tree Pipits need only the minimum of cover to conceal their nest, and a nearby perch for the male bird to dance into the air from, and descend fluttering as he utters his song. They may become unwilling foster parents for a nestling Cuckoo (plate 58).

Any bared ground is quickly colonised by plants, Foxgloves usually giving the first splash of colour, followed by Rosebay Willow-herb. Grasses, other herbs and shrubs all spring up and compete with the planted trees. The situation is now ideal for many of our small song birds. During spring and early summer Grasshopper Warblers reel incessantly, Whitethroats alarm, while both Willow Warbler and Chiffchaff utter their distinctive songs.

The high-pitched squeaking of Common and Pygmy Shrews indicates many a battle among the grass stems, while overhead Kestrels hover ever-watchful for the unwary Short-tailed Vole that ventures into the open.

As the crop grows so does the accompanying vegetation providing ideal cover for a host of wild life. Into this the Rabbit will creep after a night's feeding on the more recently-planted areas. Myxamatosis hit the forest rabbits hard around 1954, but despite sporadic outbreaks since, rabbit numbers appear to be building up once more and again cause problems for the Rangers whose job it is to protect the growing tree crop. Stoats also declined in numbers when the rabbit population fell, and are now far less common. Weasels, those most ferocious of hunters, however take advantage of the cover provided by the thicket crops. Bank Voles find the situation to their liking, and occasionally the compact grass-ball nests of Dormice are found.

Eventually with careful tending the planted trees suppress the other vegetation and form a thick impenetrable plantation. It is the warmth of these plantations that wintering flocks of Redwing and Fieldfare seek after a day's foraging over open meadows, and in which the Turtle Dove in summer builds its flimsy nest. As the growing trees now compete with one another, the forester at intervals throughout the rest of the crop's life carries out thinnings. This gradual opening up again lets in the light and clumps of vegetation grow once more on the forest floor. Woodcock that flit over the trees on their 'roding' flights nest under these pole-stage plantations. A sitting bird is almost invisible, so well does it blend with its surroundings. Sparrow Hawks, of which a few pairs still exist in the Forest, sometimes nest among the branches of a larch. The diminutive Goldcrest, that smallest of all British birds, hangs its beautiful nest in the branches of a spruce.

As the trees again grow towards maturity, they provide safe nesting sites for larger birds. Buzzards whose mewing cries can still be heard as they soar high over the tree tops, and Carrion Crows with their sheep-wool-lined nests. Grey Squirrels chatter and scold, having now completely replaced the Red Squirrel which was last seen in the area in the late 1930's.

It has been said that 'Good forestry is good conservation'. The preceding paragraphs have indicated how the work of the forester enriches the variety of wild life by the creation of varying habitats. Whether it is the relatively short rotation of a conifer crop or the longer one of a hardwood, or one of the many permutations in between, the forest is a living thing, constantly changing season by season, year by year.

Traditionally the Forest of Dean is an oak forest. Although today many areas have been planted with conifers, much oak woodland remains. With over 300 insects dependent on the oak, it is the most important component of the British woodland scene. These insects provide a vital link in that all-important food chain.

Whether they hide among the many lichen species, or in the oak bark, or feed among the foliage, insects are eagerly sought by a host of birds. Tree Creepers creep mouse-like up the trunk, searching every cranny, while the hatching of many oak woodland nesting birds coincides with the main larval infestation of the oak crowns. Blue Tits, Great Tits, Redstarts and many more collect repeated beakfulls to satisfy their ever hungry broods. Often when the oak crowns are plagued with the caterpillars of the Oak Roller Moth, multitudes of Starlings, Jackdaws and Rooks from nearby village colonies invade the tree tops to enjoy the welcome feast. Old oaks with their numerous holes provide safe nesting sites, for among others, Tawny Owls, and Nuthatches who reduce their nest's entrance by mud plastering. Noctule, Pipistrelle and Long-Eared Bats roost in such holes, while mice will fill them with acorns as a winter larder in the autumn. The acorns are also eagerly sought by a wide variety of creatures. Jays carry them off to bury, Fallow Deer gorge on them, while Wood Pigeons, in vast winter flocks, stuff their crops until almost unable to fly. The oak fulfils many other functions in the forest community. The heavy leaf fall in autumn enriches the soil below, through which Moles tunnel in their relentless search for worms. Wood Warblers, who feed and sing among the crowns, nest on the floor below, and the careful observer may catch sight of a Lesser Spotted Woodpecker working along a branch.

One interesting summer visitor very dependent on oak woodland, and has a strong breeding population in the Forest of Dean, is the Pied Flycatcher. Being a hole nester, it has readily taken to nest boxes provided in a number of areas. Each year the chicks are ringed, and a few have subsequently been recovered from or en route to their wintering grounds in Southern Europe and North Africa. Many other species breed regularly in the boxes, the most usual being Blue and Great Tits, while Coal and Marsh Tits, Redstarts, Nuthatches, Tree Creepers and Wrens have all been recorded. Occasionally the occupied boxes are raided by both Great Spotted Woodpeckers and Weasels. Wood Mice, and the larger more aggressive Yellow-necked Mice, regularly raise families in them, and in one locality Dormice Pipistrelle, and Long-Eared Bats occasionally roost, and on at least one occasion a Pygmy Shrew has been found in a bird nest box. Tawny Owls will use suitable boxes.

Although woodland covers much of that wedge of land between the Severn and Wye, the naturalist will find many other interesting habitats. Much of the land is agricultural interspersed with orchards. Here Hares can be seen on the open fields, while around hedgerows and in orchards Little Owls and Tree Sparrows are typical. Forest villages and small towns provide yet another habitat. On warm thundery summer evenings, screaming Swifts cleave the air, while wandering Hedgehogs are in constant danger on the busy roads. In winter, flocks of Chaffinches, Greenfinches and very occasionally a Brambling throng around the bird table, and the unobtrusive Dunnock will quietly feed in the vegetable patch.

Man's industrial activity has created most of the Dean's unique character. Deep in old iron workings, some dating from Roman times, the caver will find clusters of Greater Horseshoe Bats, and the less

Otter and salmon

47

gregarious Lesser Horseshoe. Nearer the mine entrance Natterer's Bat may be found. On the waste land where spoil from the forest mines was once tipped, Meadow Pipits make their home, while boggy patches attract Reed Buntings. Once the Woodlark was common, but now only odd birds are recorded.

Into the soft earth of older tree-covered tips, Badgers dig their setts. Seen only by those who watch quietly at dusk, or spotted briefly in a headlight, they are common throughout the Forest.

Numerous quarries prove a haven for wild life. Kestrels and the occasional Raven nest on the steep faces, while Stock Doves and Jackdaws make their homes in cracks and crevices. Where unwanted quarry stone has been tipped, a Vixen may raise her cubs, and the invading gorse provides cover for the nests of Yellow Hammers, Linnets and that most beautiful of all constructions, the nest of the Long-Tailed Tit.

Numerous small streams run through the forest, along which Dipper and Grey Wagtail may be found. In winter streamside alders attract flocks of Siskin and Redpoll, while in spring well-rotted branches provide soft going for the Willow Tit to excavate a nest hole.

The forest ponds, which so attract the visitor, also draw the wild life. At Noxon a party of Whooper Swans have been resident throughout past winters, while odd Goldeneye, Pochard, and Tufted Duck turn up at Cannop. The visitor to Soudley Pond may see the blue flash of a Kingfisher as it speeds away to a safer perch, or catch sight of a Little Grebe before it bobs under water. Mallard occur on all forest ponds, and the odd Shoveller or Teal may be seen.

Many of the smaller ponds attract large numbers of gum-booted children in the spring, who, armed with jam jars, capture the courting newts. All three species, Smooth, Palmate and the dragon-like Warty newt are all to be found. Common Frogs and Toads (plate 54) spawn in the shallows, providing a welcome meal for the marauding Grass Snake. The poisonous Adder is only locally common in the forest (plate 48).Common Lizard and the snake-like Slow Worm make up the reptile list (plates 53 and 55).

One cannot write about the Forest of Dean without discussing the River Severn. With its vast low-tide flats and wide riverside meadows, it enriches the wealth and variety of the area's wild life. The Otter, once common along both the Wye and Severn, has seldom been recorded in recent years, but both Grey and Common Seal have been described. Those other inshore sea mammals Dolphins and Porpoises have been spotted in the Severn on odd occasions. In winter large Wigeon flocks gather, Golden Plover join the Lapwing, and the occasional gaggle of White-fronted Geese drops down to graze. The mud flats become white with Gulls as they fly in to roost, all five common species being represented. In early spring the Lapwing begin their tumbling display flights, Redshank pipe incessantly, while passing Common Sandpipers bob at the water's edge. Yellow Wagtail and Wheatear are among the earliest migrants to pass through, and usually during April Whimbrel can be found among the Curlews. Throughout the summer Reed and Sedge Warblers sing from the reed-lined drains, and Water Voles plop into the water at the first sign of danger. During late summer the wader flocks begin to gather and by autumn hundreds of Dunlin are to be found feeding on the meadows at high tide. Ringed Plover, Turnstone and Curlew all occur in good numbers, while a wide variety of other waders including Greenshank, Grey Plover, Green Sandpiper, Ruff, Little Stint, and Curlew Sandpiper all pass through.

In a few paragraphs the wild life of this unique area can only be briefly covered. The curious and inquiring observer will find much more of equal interest. It may be a Heron stalking along a forest pond, a Shelduck leading her brood down to the Severn or the chip-chip of a passing Crossbill. Whatever it is, the Forest of Dean provides both resident and visitor with a wide variety of wild life in one of Britain's most beautiful settings.

And many a charming truth will I discover,
How birds after a wetting in the rain,
Can make their notes come twice as sweet; and then
How sparrows hop with both their legs together
While pigeons stride leg after leg, like men.

The Song of Life   W.H.Davies

Bats in the Forest of Dean

J.J.Walling

The bats, as a group, have been much neglected by field-naturalists and there are many gaps in our knowledge concerning this aspect of the Forest fauna. Up to the present there are definite records for seven of the twelve species which occur in the British Isles. Further research will almost certainly increase this total.

The Noctule is a woodland bat and has been found at Coleford and the Nagshead plantation. In deciduous woods it sometimes roosts in large numbers in disused woodpecker holes. At Nagshead more than a hundred of these large bats were seen to emerge from such a roosting place.

Although the Pipistrelle is said to be our commonest bat, records from the Forest are few. It appears to be closely associated with human habitations and has been identified at Cinderford and Parkend. Only one record exists for the Whiskered Bat—again from Coleford where a small colony inhabits an old mine tunnel.

The Long-eared Bat is another woodland species which occurs especially in deciduous tracts. Evidence of its presence can be found in rock recesses in the Forest's disused quarries in the shape of discarded wings of moths, especially the Yellow Underwing.

One of the rare British bats, the Barbastelle, is likewise associated with deciduous trees and the only Forest record is of a small colony of six found under the loose bark of an oak at Nagshead.

Finally we find numerous specimens of the cave-loving Horseshoe bats, both Lesser and Greater, in the 'scowles' at Aylburton and Coleford (plate 47).

Insect Life

O. P. Clarkson Webb

The Dean Forest and Wye Valley embraces a great variety of
habitats ranging from tidal rivers to high forest, with many intermediate stages, some of which, such as disused mine workings and
quarries, have been strongly influenced by man's activities. Each
type of habitat is the home of insects more or less specialised in their
requirements, and the richness of insect life in the area is largely due
to the exceptional variety of habitats available.

There was indeed a tendency in post-war forestry practice to reduce
this variety by planting large areas with one species of tree, such as
spruce, larch or oak, but it is now recognised that mixed plantings
have many advantages and in this case, as in others, the interests of
good forestry and of wildlife conservation coincide.

Rivers, lakes, pools, bogs, various types of grassland, heathland,
broad-leaved forest and coniferous forest all contribute their quota to
the number of insect species to be found in our area, and even the
most casual visitor, if he is not immovably car-bound, will see during
the summer months some of the largest and most beautiful insects in
Britain. If we begin from our main rivers and work upwards and
outwards through different types of habitat to the high forest zone on
either side of the River Wye, we may see in their season all the most
conspicuous insects of the forest.

Rivers and streams

Of our forty-three native species of dragonflies only six show a
marked preference for running water, and all but one of these are
found in our area. The River Wye, above the tidal reaches, supports
a number of these species, especially in the neighbourhood of
Symonds Yat. The Banded Agrion is found here, a large damselfly
with a slow fluttering flight, distinguished by its rich blue body and
its wings partially shaded dark blue. The female has a brilliant
metallic-green body with yellow-shaded wings.

The damselflies are easily told apart from the dragonflies proper
by their graceful fluttering flight and their habit of folding their
wings over their backs when at rest instead of keeping them horizon-
tally extended. Accompanying the Banded Agrion on the riverbank
may be some of the smaller sky-blue bodied damselflies such as the
White-legged Damselfly, of which the male dangles his white legs in
front of the female in something resembling a courtship display.

Many of the forest streams are too polluted for most insect life,
but here and there the Demoiselle Agrion maintains a precarious
foothold, a species similar to the Banded Agrion but with its wings

wholly shaded dark blue. Beside swift upland streams the striking Golden-ringed Dragonfly can occasionally be seen. This is the largest of our native dragonflies and the female has an exceptionally long ovipositor which she uses to ram her eggs into the stony bed of a stream. Plates 44 and 45 show a dragonfly and a damselfly respectively.

Lakes and pools

Past industries often required the damming-up of streams to form ponds, of which there are many examples, and opencast mining has often left pools which are rich in insect life.

The gorgeous blue-striped Emperor Dragonfly is conspicuous in June and July as it hawks up and down many ponds in the eastern half of the forest. It is a voracious predator on smaller insects, and it is a normal experience to see, and hear, one of them crunching up a butterfly in the air and letting its wings flutter to the water.

The Broad-bodied Libellula, of which the mature male is brilliant blue and the female brown and yellow, is equally conspicuous at some ponds in June and July, while at others (the two species seldom frequent the same pond) it is replaced by the brown, slightly smaller, Four-Spot Libellula. These two dragonflies, instead of hawking up and down a chosen beat, choose a favourite perch and dart off periodically at smaller insects.

By mid August the early summer dragonflies have been replaced by the smaller red Sympetrum dragonflies and by the big blue or green-spotted Aeshnas. The males of all our dragonflies jealously guard their chosen territories, chasing off any rival males and attempting to mate with any female which appears. On warm summer evenings up to fourteen of the big Aeshnas have been seen performing wild aerobatics over a small pond until long after sunset. Sometimes a clashing of wings can be heard in the rushes as a female Aeshna seeks a suitable place along the water's edge where she can lay her eggs in the tissues of plants. The females of other species, such as the Libellulas and the Sympetrums, hover over the surface of the water dipping their abdomen repeatedly into the water and washing the eggs off so that they sink to the bottom.

At most of the forest pools the small red or blue damselflies can be seen swarming over the surface throughout the summer, often attracting swallows and martins in search of an easy meal.

The Forest of Dean is fortunate to have fresh water available for these strikingly attractive insects, but the future is not so bright. Many ponds have already been filled in or used as dumps for rubber tyres, old cars or other refuse. Others have been allowed to dry out or become overgrown. Some form of protection is urgently needed for the best surviving examples, and encouragement should be given to the young people who show themselves willing to do the arduous job of clearance.

SYMONDS YAT,
MONMOUTH
and COLEFORD

MILES

HIGH
MEADOW

D••

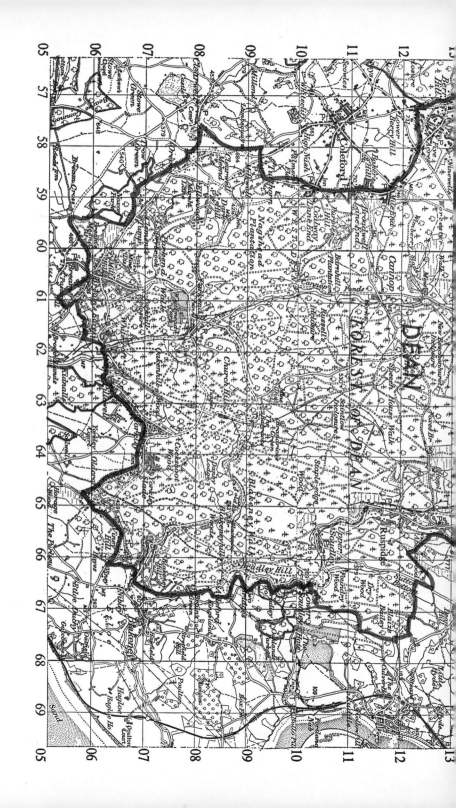

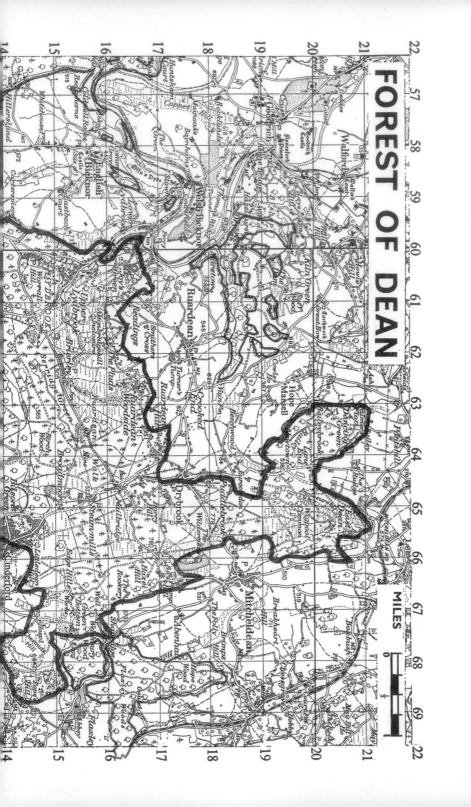

FOREST OF DEAN

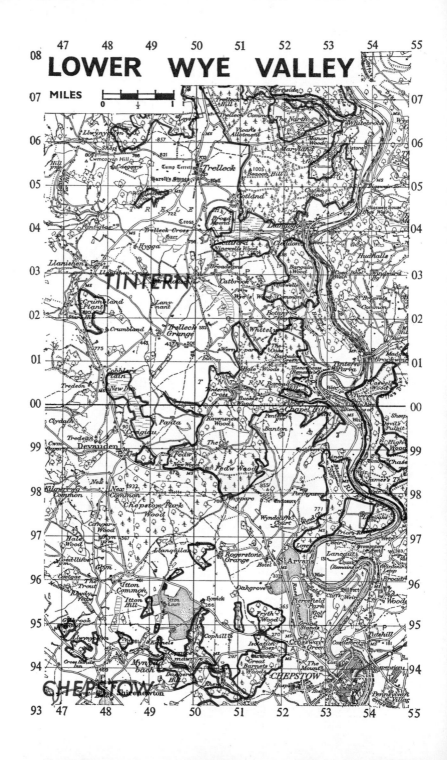

LOWER WYE VALLEY

Grassland and heathland

Permanent grassland, especially if it lies over calcareous rocks, supports a large variety of insects. The hillocks of the Yellow Hill Ant often form a conspicuous feature of calcareous grassland: these are built up of soil particles carried up from the nest itself which may be some distance from the hillock. These hillocks often provide homes for grasshoppers in their early stages, particularly the Meadow Grasshopper, one of our commoner species, which is easily recognised by its inability to fly: its wings are small and virtually useless, but it is a respectable jumper. Other common grasshoppers in our area are the Common Field and the Common Green grasshoppers. Colour is not usually a reliable guide to identification, but most grasshoppers are best identified by their 'song', or stridulation, which is produced by rubbing the hind legs against the fore wings. The Common Green Grasshopper produces a prolonged loud ticking for up to 20 seconds, while the Common Field Grasshopper can only produce short chirps at intervals of 1 or 2 seconds.

Disused railway-tracks and spoil-heaps form an important habitat for butterflies as well as grasshoppers. The Grayling butterfly is especially characteristic of such places and occurs where there is bare ground or short turf with tufts of Sheep's Fescue grass. This butterfly's habit of 'disappearing' by settling on the ground, closing its wings and tilting them so as to avoid casting a shadow, is one of the most entertaining tricks in nature.

Another butterfly skilled at disappearing is the Wall Brown, which is particularly partial to sunny banks on which it settles, shutting its wings with a jerk whenever danger threatens. In late spring, when it first appears, it is often seen flying with the little grey-and-white Grizzled Skipper, the Dingy Skipper, the Common Blue and the dashing little Small Copper.

In high summer the same butterflies re-appear, except the two Skippers, and are joined by other Browns and Skippers, together with the day-flying Burnet moths. Here and there a large tawny-brown butterfly dashing wildly over the ground may turn out to be the Dark Green Fritillary, one of our strongest fliers.

Beetles are numerous wherever there is sufficient cover, for they are fond of camouflaging their presence. One of the largest and commonest, the Cockchafer or Maybug, can often be discovered

Rhagium Beetles

trying to batter its way into well-lit houses during late spring evenings. The Tiger Beetle is an active predator of smaller insects, running about sunny banks in the spring months. Red Soldier beetles are often abundant in open situations and recently a large dark-blue species of Soldier beetle has been discovered in our area which was previously known only from Derbyshire northwards, where it was considered rare.

Glowworms used to be frequent, but have recently been reported only from one disused railway track on the forest outskirts. The Devil's Coach-horse is a villainous-looking black wingless beetle which twists its tail up over its back like a scorpion when danger threatens, but is in fact harmless to humans. The Rhagium beetles are active green or grey insects with long bodies and antennae. They fly about in sunlight and are often seen on gates and stiles.

The few remaining tracts of heathland, such as that on Tidenham Chase, support many of the grassland insects with the addition of some, such as the day-flying Fox Moth and the Mottled Grasshopper, which show a preference for heathland.

The permanent grassland area is constantly diminishing as railway tracks are resurfaced to take heavy forestry equipment, old spoil tips are planted with conifers and natural grassland is ploughed and sown to ryegrass mixtures. These developments may be inevitable, but the price paid in loss of wildlife is often only realised too late.

Woodland

In many parts of the Dean Forest and Wye Valley, especially where there are immature plantations of a single species over a large area, the insect life is poor. If however attention is concentrated on mature deciduous or mixed woodland with plenty of sheltered grassy rides, a great wealth of insects can be seen, and of these the most conspicuous are the butterflies.

In May the tawny Black-spotted Pearl-Bordered Fritillary patrols sunny woodland rides wherever there are Bugle flowers and Dog Violets growing nearby, the latter being the larval foodplant. In the damper areas such as on Wigpool Common and at Trelech Bog it is replaced by the Small Pearl-Bordered Fritillary which has darker markings on the underside of the wings.

By the end of June the magnificent Silver-Washed Fritillary is on the wing, its majestic gliding-and-dipping flight fascinating to watch as it searches for the bramble blossoms on which it feeds. It appears to roost high in the trees, for a short spell of warm sunshine will bring it floating down from the tops of trees. The female, in her search for suitable egg-laying sites, will enter the darkest woods in order to lay her eggs in the crevices of a tree trunk at a height of three to six feet from the ground; in the spring the young larva will crawl to the ground to feed on the Dog Violet leaves which it finds below.

Another of our fine woodland butterflies is the White Admiral, which is still to be found in a few localities where the forester has left some of its larval foodplant, the Honeysuckle. The flight of this gorgeous black-and-white insect is the most graceful thing imaginable, but its fondness for bramble blossoms often makes it an easy prey for the collector.

The third of our trio of fine woodland butterflies, the Purple Emperor, has not been seen in the Forest for thirty years and may have disappeared owing to felling of its habitat, mature oakwood with sallow understorey. Its place has largely been taken by other Vanessids such as the Comma, a swift jagged-winged brown butterfly with black markings (plate 46). The underside of the wings is sooty-black except for a white mark like a comma. The larva, when at rest on the nettle leaves on which it feeds, looks like a bird dropping.

Other Vanessids such as the Peacock, Small Tortoishell and Red Admiral are familiar on the Buddleia shrubs in our gardens, although they are also woodland insects. The graceful yellow Brimstone, usually the first butterfly to appear in the spring, is rather variable in numbers, but its foodplant, the Alder Buckthorn, is common on Tidenham Chase where it is carefully preserved as a kind of nursery for the larvae when the butterfly falls on hard times elsewhere.

Three species of Hairstreak butterflies occur locally. These small butterflies all have a narrow white line on the underside of the wings. The Green Hairstreak prefers open spaces near water and can be seen dashing up and down its territory in May and June. The Purple Hairstreak has a lovely purple sheen on the upper side of its wings but it normally keeps to the tops of oak trees except when it is attracted to bramble blossoms lower down. The White-Letter Hairstreak has a

Ichneumon fly laying an egg to parasitise a wood wasp grub hidden beneath pine bark.

similar liking for the tops of elm trees, but seems to be attracted to privet as well as bramble.

The woodland moths, except for the day-flying Silver Y Moth, are less often seen owing to their nocturnal habits, but a number of the active Hawk Moths are found in this area. Some of them, such as the small Humming-Bird Hawk Moths which are sometimes seen hovering before strongly-scented flowers at dusk in Wye Valley gardens, are immigrants from abroad, but others, such as the Privet, Poplar, Lime and Large Elephant Hawk, Moths are undoubtedly native. The Rosebay Willowherb, or Fireweed, is the main foodplant of the larva of the latter species, a fearsome-looking dark-grey creature with two pairs of markings like eyes just behind the head; it is nevertheless easy and rewarding to rear in captivity (plate 43).

Of special interest to the entomologist are two rare moths, the Scarce Hook-tip and Fletcher's Pug, which were discovered in the Lower Wye Valley in 1961–2.

On warm summer evenings and often during the day when it is dull and close, Bush Crickets are to be seen on the margins of woodland and in scrubby areas. They are related to grasshoppers but are generally bulkier and have long waving antennae. The females are distinguished by the long, upward-curving ovipositor at the rear tip of the body. One of the commonest, the Dark Bush Cricket, is flightless and frequently enters houses where it can be mistaken for a spider until one notices its six legs. Other species commonly found in the forest are the Speckled and Oak Bush Crickets, both being an attractive green. They are all partly carnivorous, feeding on smaller insects, whereas the grasshoppers are strictly vegetarian. The chirping of the House Cricket used to be a familiar sound to many households, but with modern standards of hygiene it has become distinctly scarce. However, it still survives in one remarkable site, a disused spoil-tip which for at least thirty years has maintained a high temperature by spontaneous combustion of the waste materials within.

The number of woodland insects is so large, if one were to include the ants, bees, wasps, hoverflies, true flies, bugs etc., that this account could be extended indefinitely. However, one cannot omit the Wood Ant, the largest of our species, whose nests consisting of heaps of pine needles, leaves or twigs sometimes reach a height of a metre or more. It is quite easy to follow the main lines of traffic to and from their nests and the rustle of their moving feet on the dead leaves is quite audible on a warm, quiet day. Like other social insects, ants frequently harbour 'lodgers' in the form of other insects which may or may not be parasites. Two uncommon species of beetle have been found in Wood Ant nests in our area, one of which certainly preys on the young ants.

All things considered, the present wealth of insects in our woodland is unlikely to be seriously threatened as long as a wide variety of trees continues to be grown to maturity and the pressures on our ponds and open spaces are successfully resisted.

I'll see again the green leaves suddenly
Turned into flowers by resting butterflies;
While all around are small, brown, working bees,
And hairy black-and-ambers, twice their size.

The Song of Life   W.H.Davies

Acknowledgement

The author gladly acknowledges help received in the preparation of this article from Mr. Austin Richardson, M.A., F.R.E.S., Dr. G.A.Neil Horton, M.A., and Mr. D.B.Atty, M.A.

57

Plant Life and Vegetation

Dr. E. W. Jones & J. M. B. Brown

The Dean Forest Park has an exceptionally interesting and varied flora. The natural occurrence of various kinds of trees and plants has been governed in part by the climate, and partly by the different rock beds and soils which will be described in the next chapter. But everywhere the hand of man has had its effect. Many of the woods that the visitor sees to-day have been purposely planted by foresters; others, though of natural origin, have been altered or influenced in their composition by the woodman's work. In those portions of the forest that are open to grazing, the sheep have checked the undergrowth, and this accounts for the absence of shrubs and young trees on many areas where they might otherwise be expected. Some of the sites occupied by plant life are actually man-made, such as the colliery tips with their interesting pioneer vegetation. Plants introduced from foreign lands occur along the streamsides, and botanists and plant-lovers will find the whole Park, which now includes a unique Ecological Reserve, a fruitful field of study.

The influence of climate

Although the Forest of Dean is only a small area, the sharp relief, with a range in altitude from sea level to around 1,000 ft., introduces a good deal of local variation in climate. There are high, exposed and cold eminences and ridges, such as Edgehills, Ruardean, Buckstone; warm sunny slopes; and damp, frosty valleys and hollows such as Cannop. On the whole, however, the forest has an equable, westerly climate, with a rainfall of about 36 ins. (more on the hills) and mean monthly temperatures ranging from 38° to 61°f; Fahrenheit; the winters are generally mild and the summers moderately warm. Climatically the district belongs to the wet warm lowlands of south-western England, but one may infer from its vegetation that it has some features of the equally wet but colder climates of the hill country of northern England. Of the rarer and more local plants which grow in the district the majority are characteristic of south-western England and south Wales: but there are one or two noteworthy occurrences of plants which are characteristic of northern England and of the mountains of central Europe (*Festuca sylvatica; Stellaria nermorum; Campanula latifolia*).

The influence of soils

The distribution of the main rock formations is shown on the geological map and described in the chapter on geology, which follows this one, with a geological map on page 68.

The central area of the forest, overlying the Coal Measures, carries soils ranging from somewhat acid sandy loams, derived from sandstones, to the clay loams and clays, derived from the shales and fireclays. The Drybrook Sandstone gives a very much poorer, more siliceous soil than the more widespread Pennant Sandstone. All the soils derived from the Coal Measures, whether from sandstones or shales, are poor in nutrients and tend to be acid: for this reason, they carry a very limited flora. The Carboniferous Limestone, forming an outcrop nearly all round the forest, as shown on the geological sketch map, gives much more fertile soils—stiff loams or clay loams, rich in nutrients: consequently they have a great variety of plants. The Old Red Sandstone, which forms the outer fringe of the Forest area, yields a deep, light, sandy loam, not unlike that derived from the Pennant Sandstone in many respects, but distinctly more fertile. The coarse conglomerates, such as form the Buckstone ridge, however, yield soils which are locally very shallow and acid; they are often characterized by abundance of the Great Woodrush (*Luzula sylvatica*). In general, as far as rate of growth and size are concerned, the Old Red Sandstone soils are the best for tree-growth. When deep enough, the soils from Carboniferous Limestone and Pennant Sandstone are little inferior, but over these rocks the soil is often very shallow, and growth is then very poor. The soils from the Drybrook Sandstone are the poorest.

As far as variety of species is concerned the Carboniferous Limestone is much the richest, and many rare and local species, which are confined in Britain to the limestone of the South West (e.g. the Mendips and Glamorgan) are to be found here. The Wye Gorge, around and below Symonds Yat, in the High Meadow Woods, forms the largest and best area for the study of this fascinating flora; there is another limestone area forming part of Wigpool Common, whilst the limestone areas of Tidenham Chase and the Wye Valley between Tintern and Chepstow are also of considerable interest. Wigpool Common and Tidenham Chase are also noteworthy for their outcrops of acid sandy soils of the Drybrook Sandstone type.

The trees and their history

The present condition of the Forest is largely due to man—even the existing oak has mostly been planted—and one can only guess what it would be like in the absence of human interference.

OAK would certainly have been a very important species, though it would have been far less conspicuous than it is to-day. There are two species, the Common or Pedunculate oak (*Quercus robur*) and the Sessile or Durmast oak (*Quercus petraea*). The former is to be distinguished by the long stalks to the acorn-cups (to which the name refers) and by the very short leaf-stalks. The durmast oak, which is a tree

59

of more limited distribution, grows rather taller, with a straighter trunk, and has acorns clustered directly on the twigs or on very short stalks, and leaf-stalks about half an inch long: the back of the leaf is distinctly hairy, particularly along the main vein. The leaf is more regularly and less deeply lobed than in pedunculate oak. There is much evidence to show that the sessile oak was originally the principal species in the Forest and that the pedunculate oak has, for the most part, been deliberately planted, under the mistaken impression that it was the more valuable species for timber. Both species are natives and hybrids occur abundantly. The famous Newland Oak, which grew in a pasture about one mile north-west of Newland Church, was a pollard tree with the greatest girth recorded in modern times for any tree in Britain—namely forty-four feet. Unfortunately this veteran collapsed, through the decay of its heart-wood, early in 1955 (Oak appears in plates 2 and 17).

BEECH (*Fagus sylvatica*) has long been recognised as being a native on the steep, rocky slopes of the Wye Valley, and for many years it was believed that this was the westernmost of the several limited areas where beech was a genuinely 'wild' tree. However, it is now certain that it was once abundant throughout Southern Britain, having in most places been eliminated by man, since its seedlings are very palatable to his grazing animals. In the primeval Forest of Dean, beech would certainly have been at least as abundant and conspicuous as oak. Much beech has been deliberately planted in the Forest during relatively recent years; but old beech still occurs on the sandy soils (Old Red Sandstone) at Danby Lodge and Blaize Bailey, as well as in the High Meadow Woods. (Plates 3 and 4).

SWEET CHESTNUT (*Castanea sativa*) is generally believed to have been brought in by the Romans, who used its nuts for food. It was much planted here and elsewhere in the first quarter of the last century; but Flaxley Abbey was granted a share in a wood of chestnut as long ago as the reign of Henry II (*c.* 1170) and chestnuts are common in the Flaxley Woods to this day. At present chestnut occurs occasionally mixed with oak in some woods and also forms some beautiful pure woods—to some extent depleted during the war— where the soil is dry and deep, as at Chestnuts Inclosure near Littledean, and near the former New Fancy Colliery.

In the primeval forests on the Limestone, ASH (*Fraxinus excelsior*) would have been as abundant and conspicuous as oak. Yew and holly would have formed an understory and lime, elm, maple and many other trees would have been frequent.

On the sandstone soils there would have been few species other than oak and beech. Birch would have been abundant, colonising ground which had been burned, or open places where old trees had died or been blown down, later to be replaced by oak and beech,

Plate 17. Oakwood

Plate 18. Cycling through the woods, near Blakeney

Plate 19. Woodland car park

Plate 20. East of Pleasant Stile, near Newnham, the mighty Severn winds seawards

Plate 21. Evening sunlight on a typical Dean farmstead, in the Flaxley Valley

Plate 22. Cannop Pond

Plate 23. Caravanners

Plate 24. The Biblins Adventure Centre, near Symonds Yat

germinating in its shade. Mountain ash would have been frequent and holly might well have formed a dense understory. The celebrated hollies of Holly Wood near Speech House are said to have been planted in the seventeenth century; some are six feet in girth.

The CONIFERS are distinguished by producing their seeds in cones and by having needle-shaped leaves. All the common conifers grown in Britain are evergreen, except the larch (*Larix decidua*), which was introduced from the Italian Alps in 1629 as an ornamental but scarcely used as a timber tree in England for another century. Some fine larch trees have been grown in the Forest of Dean at Lea Bailey, Braceland, and in the High Meadow Woods, including specimens well over 100 ft. high. The Braceland larch, planted about 1825, measured 9 ft. 3 in. in girth at breast height in 1897, and 12 ft. 4 in. in 1946.

The Limestone soils

On the Limestone there is a great mixture of species. Ash is often abundant and oak relatively rare: beech is common and luxuriant in all the older woodland. Lime (*Tilia cordata*, the Small-leaved lime, and *Tilia platyphyllos*, the Broad-leaved lime) and Wych elm are often very abundant and grow from coppice. The wild service (*Sorbus torminalis*) with its superb autumn colouring, and the lovely white-beam (*Sorbus aria*) with its silvery-grey leaves, are frequent. Often dog's mercury, mingled with wood anemone and bluebell, covers the ground where shade is deep. With greater light, blackberries and wild rose (*Rosa arvensis*) become abundant. On cool, stony slopes in deep shade the hart's tongue fern often covers the ground, while in moister places garlic (*Allium ursinum*) may form carpets. In May its sheets of white blossom make a display less familiar than that of the bluebell but just as spectacular. Woodruff (*Asperula odorata*) is also conspicuous at this time. Yews mark the stony patches of shallow soil and cling to the cliffs. The jutting limestone promontories of the Wye Gorge are often capped by a soil which is so thin and dry that it is insufficient to support anything but a very poor and open scrub: on top of these sunny promontories are some of the rarest plants of the district. There are relatively few plantations on the Limestone. In the early years, while the young crop is still open, blackberry and wild rose are often very abundant, and together with privet, hawthorn and blackthorn help to make the forester's job difficult. Limestone grassland, which is gay in June and July with rock rose (*Helianthemum vulgare*) and thyme (*Thymus serpyllum*), only occurs to a small extent on the larger rides and on the rocky promontories in High Meadow Woods: it is rather more extensive, however, on Wigpool Common and Tidenham Chase and may be seen also in the old limestone quarries throughout the district. Rarer plants include the toothwort (*Lathraea squamaria*) and the stinking hellebore (*Helleborus foetidus*).

Coal Measure areas

On the Coal Measure sandstones and clays, widely-spaced pure oak, planted in the period 1800–1825, is the commonest crop. Beneath this the ground is often covered with bracken and grasses (*Deschampsia flexuosa, Holcus mollis*), the proportion depending very much on the amount of grazing. Sheep also prevent any undergrowth of shrubs from developing and keep down the blackberries. Some of the woods have been enclosed and underplanted with beech during the past forty or fifty years. Beech is also abundant in the High Meadow Woods and Abbots Wood, where there is no grazing and the ground is generally covered with blackberry, mixed with grasses and a few herbaceous species (*Holcus mollis, Lamium galeobdolon, Stellaria holostea, Oxalis acetosella*). The poorer and more acid soils, such as those derived from Drybrook Sandstone, are often marked by abundance of bilberry and heath bedstraw, by carpets of the grass *Deschampsia flexuosa*, or mosses (*Polytrichum formosum, Hypnum cupressiforme, Dicranum scoparium*), and by grey, rounded cushions of the moss *Leucobryum glaucum*.

Large areas of the Coal Measure soil have been converted to conifer plantations in the past; and the changes associated with the changing crop form an interesting study. In the early stages after the felling of old woods, foxgloves, rose-bay willow herb, marsh plume-thistle, and St. John's wort are often very abundant and with their blaze of colour provide ample compensation for the loss of the trees. Bracken may become tall and dense and have to be cut by the forester, and broom and gorse often invade the plantation. As the young crops close and provide dense shade, these plants disappear, and beneath Norway spruce and Douglas fir the ground will become wholly bare. As the crop ages the light increases once more and shade-loving plants, especially the bluebell and the dainty wood-sorrel, enter. Plantations during this phase offer the finest display of bluebells. With advancing age and increasing light, bracken, bilberry and grasses will regain their hold. Felling and replanting, partly with oak and other hardwoods, partly with conifers, occurred at an accelerated pace from 1939–1955 and the consequent changes in the vegetation are everywhere visible.

Rides, paths and glades

This habitat provides an opening for such herbs as need more light than the woods usually give, and the vegetation is often very luxuriant. In the wetter places, as along the rides, flourish marsh plumethistle (*Cirsium palustre*), lesser skullcap (*Scutellaria minor*), marsh bedstraw (*Galium palustre*), hard rush (*Juncus inflexus*), tufted hairgrass (*Deschampsia caespitosa*), creeping soft-grass (*Holcus mollis*). On the drier banks grow milkwort (*Polygala vulgaris*), greater stitchwort (*Stellaria holostea*) St. John's wort (*Hypericum perforatum*), tormentil (*Potentilla tormentilla*), yellow pimpernel (*Lysimachia vulgaris*), bilberry (*Vaccinium myrtillus*), heather (*Calluna vulgaris*), bell heather (*Erica cinerea*), speedwell (*Veronica* spp), foxglove (*Digitalis purpurea*), and sheep's sorrel (*Rumex acetosella*).

Heath vegetation

Wigpool Common and Tidenham Chase on Drybrook Sandstone provide the only examples of true heath, dominated by heather and gorse, but on thin upland sandy soils in various places occurs a form of grass-heath dominated by wavy hair grass (*Deschampsia flexuosa*), heath bedstraw (*Galium saxatile*), sheep's sorrel (*Rumex acetosella*), common agrostis (*Agrostis tenuis*), tormentil (*Potentilla tormentilla*) and bracken (*Pteridium aquilinum*). Limited areas of these heaths are to be retained in their present condition to preserve this vegetation type.

Marshes and bogs

Marshes are not frequent on the Coal Measure clays. The best example of marsh vegetation is to be seen at Foxes Bridge, near Speech House (Rushy Lawn), where a good variety of water and bog plants may be found. Aquatic vegetation is best developed in Cannop Ponds. On Wigpool Common, near Mitcheldean, the remains of a Sphagnum bog harbours *Sphagnum cymbifolium* and *S. papillosum*, sundews (*Drosera rotundifolia* and *longifolia*) and bog asphodel (*Narthecium ossifragum*).

Colliery tips

These huge heaps of waste material which occur throughout the forest show different stages of the colonisation of bare soil. The first plant to appear is commonly groundsel (*Senecio vulgaris*), after which in quick succession come shepherd's purse (*Capsella bursa-pastoris*), chickweed (*Cerastium viscosum*), pearlwort (*Sagina procumbens*), sandwort (*Arenaria serpyllifolia*). Later come coltsfoot (*Tussilago farfara*), field thistle (*Cirsium arvense*) and birch seedlings.

Several of the tips have recently been planted up, largely with conifers, but interesting mixed stands including birch, alder, and rowan have sometimes developed. It is mainly the black unburnt tips that are screened by plantations; where fires have occurred, and the shale has been burnt to a red colour, it proves suitable for filling in soft ground on industrial sites, and millions of tons have been transferred from the forest to the new Spencer Steel Works near Newport.

The Old Red Sandstone zone

On the Old Red Sandstone, as on the Coal Measure sandstone, the old broad-leaved woodland is mainly of oak. Locally, especially in moist valley bottoms, a little lime and wych elm may be present and ash is a little more frequent than on the Coal Measure sandstones. In the ungrazed areas, such as the High Meadow Woods, beech is abundant. On the better soils blackberry covers the ground beneath the trees, but yields to dense bracken where the light is greater. As on the Coal Measures, bluebells are abundant in young plantations. Poorer soils, especially on steep slopes, are characterized by masses of the great woodrush (*Luzula sylvatica*), a species which occurs on Coal Measures and on limestone as well, but without attaining the same luxuriance and abundance. Rodge Wood, on the slope below the Buckstone at Staunton, is an excellent example of this kind of vegetation.

On the eastern border of the forest the wild daffodil is characteristic of woods and old pastures on the Old Red Sandstone, and in the country from Longhope to Dymock it grows in great profusion.

There are also stretches of open bracken-covered ground, such as Staunton Meend, and much of the land on the borders of the forest, as around St. Briavels and Longhope and Mayhill, is farmland, often with the fields divided up by old stone walls, on which grow ferns such as the scaly-black (*Ceterach officinarum*), flowering plants such as wall pennywort (*Cotyledon umbilicus*) and *Saxifraga tridactylites*, together with many interesting mosses and lichens. Altogether, the Old Red Sandstone country, with its pleasantly diversified topography, its finely timbered woods intermingling with farmland and old villages, together with a varied and interesting flora, forms some of the most attractive parts of the forest. All the plants found on the Coal Measures may be found on the Old Red Sandstone, for which some characteristic and rarer plants are recorded in the following list: woodrushes (*Luzula sylvatica* and *Luzula fosteri*), sedge (*Carex laevigata*), vetch (*Vicia sylvatica*) bellflower (*Campanula patula*), mountain speedwell (*Veronica montana*), wild daffodil (*Narcissus*

Foxgloves

pseudonarcissus), fescue (*Festuca sylvatica*) red currant (*Ribes rubrum*), wood stitchwort (*Stellaria nemorum*), golden saxifrages (*Chrysosplenium oppositifolium* and *C. alternifolium*), hard fern (*Blechnum spicant*).

Ferns

In the district as a whole, ferns are often abundant, and in shady, disused stone quarries and moist valley bottoms are sometimes very luxuriant. All the commoner species are to be found, though some, such as the oak fern (*Polypodium dryopteris*), have been very nearly exterminated. The district is also exceptionally rich in mosses and liverworts. The Carboniferous Limestone and the Old Red Sandstone on the western margins of the forest yield by far the greater number of these and those interested should consult a paper by Miss E. Armitage in the *Journal of Ecology*, Vol II, 1914, or study the late H. H. Knight's collection of Gloucestershire mosses and liverworts in the Cheltenham Museum.

Riverside vegetation

Throughout the greater part of its course past the forest the banks of the Wye are formed by Old Red Sandstone. Although the river is not tidal above the vicinity of Monmouth, the banks are steep and muddy, for in times of flood the river rises many feet and is very swift. For this reason the aquatic vegetation is scanty. Clumps of alder are scattered along the bank, on which grow reed grass (*Phalaris arundinacea*), water dropwort (*Oenanthe crocata*), and butter-bur (*Petasites vulgaris*). Locally the snowdrop is abundant: it is, however, always near old cottage sites. Three introduced plants are naturalized along the river banks. The tall pink and white balsam from America (*Impatiens glandulifera*) occurs in places, while locally a dainty little veronica—*v. filiformis*—from eastern Europe makes bright blue patches in the turf. Another alien is the Monkey Flower (*Mimulus langsdorfii*), with bright yellow blossoms.

The High Meadow Ecological Reserve

It has been seen that the limestone woodland is especially rich in plants of every kind. There are good reasons for believing that much of the ground on the steep slopes of the Wye Valley, in the High Meadow Woods, has been woodland from time immemorial, having never been completely cleared of trees and devoted to other uses. The explanation of its richness in plants lies to some extent in this fact, as well as in local peculiarities of climate and site, e.g. the presence of natural limestone rock outcrops. The species present may thus be taken to be those pertaining to the primeval woodland of this district though man has greatly modified their relative abundance and also the form of the forest. In order to safeguard an example of this exceptionally interesting type of woodland and, still more important,

The Silver Severn

obtain information about the kind of woodland which would develop in the absence of human interference, an area of about 90 acres in Lady Park Wood, in the Highmeadow Woods above the Wye, was set aside in 1944 as an 'Ecological Reserve'. Since then, no planting operations of any sort have been carried out in the Reserve and the changes taking place are carefully recorded from time to time.

Before the 1939–45 war the last important felling in the area for many years was round about 1907, when all the smaller stems were coppiced and many old trees cut, but many more left as standards. A little thinning was later carried out from time to time. During the period 1939–45 about half of the Reserve remained untouched, except for the felling of some large lime, mainly from the lower slopes. Over the remainder of the area all the smaller stems—mainly coppice stems of ash, elm and lime arising from the 1907 felling—were cut and many of the large standards were also felled, but scattered oak and beech were left. These oak were then mostly about 150–200 years old and the beech 80–100 years. The yew was also left uncut. Coppice regrowth will form much of the new woodland which is to develop unaided after this felling, but there will also be many seedling birch, sallow and oak, perhaps beech. In the course of time the short-lived species, such as sallow and birch, will die and their place will be taken by longer-lived species. It will remain for our children and grandchildren to see how the balance of power is shared among these longer-lived species.

The banks are stormed by Speedwell, that blue flower,
  So like a little heaven with one star out;
I see an amber lake of Buttercups,
  And Hawthorn foams the hedges round about.

Seeking Beauty   W. H. Davies

The Geology of the Dean Region

B. V. Cave

Introduction

Man's history has until now been regulated by the natural processes
in and on the surface of the earth. Nowhere is this inter-relationship
of man and nature better revealed than here in the Forest of Dean.
The variety of rocks in this small area has resulted in a similar variety
of human activity. Some rocks (especially the limestones) produce
good soils and in those places are the farms and older settlements. On
the poorer soils derived from shales, clays and sandstones are situated
the forestry plantations. The coal and iron deposits in and around the
Forest have led to exploitation for the mineral wealth and resulted
in more recent settlements near mines and iron furnaces. The erosion
of the rocks has given the valleys and river systems for man's
communications.

This chapter describes how these rocks were created in the development of the earth. The oldest rocks here began as sediments laid down
over 400 million years ago on a sea bed. Repeatedly since then the
land has risen and sunk. The rocks recall these earth movements and
in their form and type tell us of the conditions of the seas under which
they were laid down and those of the surrounding land. The
sediments were pushed and crumpled in the vast pressures of the
earth's crust and now stand up revealed. More superficial deposits
that once existed have been eroded and the rocks of varying hardness
are left as hills and valleys.

A vertical slice or section from east to west across the Dean, as
shown in the drawing on pages 70 and 71, tells how the rocks are
folded beneath us and how they rise up to form the hills. The
accompanying map on page 68 shows the outcrops and rock sequence.

Silurian rocks

You will see how the oldest rocks here lying deepest in the earth rise
up to form May Hill. These are known as Silurian rocks (named
after the ancient British tribe who lived here 2,000 years ago, called
the Silures). Originally, they were formed in warm shallow seas long,
long past (400 million years ago) when the land had little vegetation
as we know it today, with only a few primitive moss-like and seaweed-
like plants in the damper places. The seas, however, had a rich plant
and animal life. Preserved coral reefs including fossils of trilobites and
brachiopods are frequent in the limestone quarries on the slopes of
May Hill. Man has used the limestone to make lime for mortar and
cement, and kilns are still to be seen in these quarries.

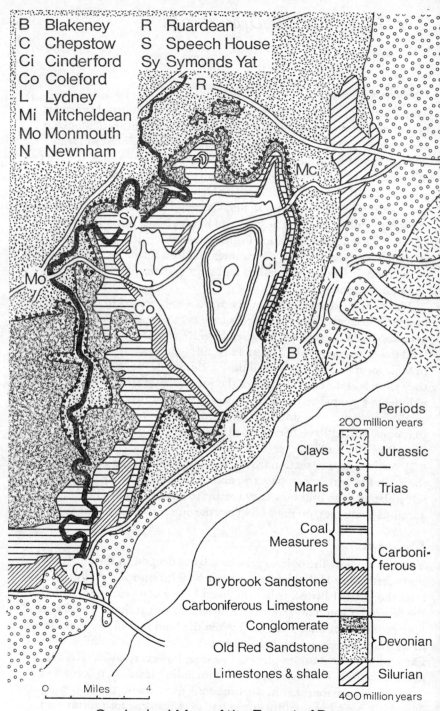

B	Blakeney
C	Chepstow
Ci	Cinderford
Co	Coleford
L	Lydney
Mi	Mitcheldean
Mo	Monmouth
N	Newnham
R	Ruardean
S	Speech House
Sy	Symonds Yat

Periods
200 million years

Clays	Jurassic
Marls	Trias
Coal Measures	Carboniferous
Drybrook Sandstone	
Carboniferous Limestone	
Conglomerate	Devonian
Old Red Sandstone	
Limestones & shale	Silurian

400 million years

O   Miles   4

Geological Map of the Forest of Dean

Plate 25. St Briavel's Castle – once a Norman bulwark against the Welsh, now a Youth Hostel

Plate 26. Chepstow Castle

Plate 27. Tintern Abbey

Plate 28. The eastward view from the Wind Cliff, near Chepstow. Here the tidal Wye makes its final curve around Lancaut and below the limestone cliffs of Wintour's Leap, to join the distant Severn at Beachley

Plate 29. All Saints Church, Staunton, with its ancient cross

Plate 30. All Saints, Newland – the Cathedral of the Forest

Plate 31. Filming

Plate 32. Swinging

Plate 33. Crawling

Plate 34. Scrambling

Plate 35. The Monnow Bridge, with its portcullised gateway, Monmouth

Plate 36. Purton Manor, a Tudor house on a cliff above the Severn, associated with Sir Walter Raleigh

The oldest rocks of May Hill, now exposed only at the very top of the hill (you can see from the diagram how this is) are sandstones. You can imagine these coarse sands laid down like a sandy beach near the land. As the land sank, coral reefs grew. As the land sank further these were submerged in beds of clay which became shales. Now again, uplifted at the present time, these beds of shales cause springs of water to emerge, because the water cannot pass through the shale and it emerges at the edges where the rock outcrops. One of the most famous springs of water in this shale bed is Royal Spring at Longhope where King Charles II is said to have rested and drank during an escape from the Roundheads. The water there is now so directed that it gushes from the side of the house.

The sea became shallower and limestone constructed of coral and other life formed again. And these again are overlain with shales.

Devonian Rocks: Old Red Sandstones and Marls

As millions of years rolled by the climate became hotter and finally red deserts surrounded the seas. Primitive ferns grew on the shores of the rivers, which flowed intermittently as rivers do today in desert regions. Amongst the shifting pools and sand bars primitive fish existed. Their remains as fossils may now be found in a few places. A number have been found in the Wilderness Quarry in the deep red sandstone on the sharp corner of the road between Mitcheldean and Longhope.

Mountains rose high in the mid-Wales region. From the desert mountains the rivers brought down cascades of red sand and clays. At times when the sea was shallow sands accumulated. At other times clays and so today far beneath the Dean are vast masses of red sandstone and red clay in alternating layers. They surface or outcrop all around. To the west they form the structures of mid-Monmouth-shire. To the east they form three ridges and valleys between Mitcheldean and May Hill. Everywhere they form good farm soils, pasture usually where they are heavier and corn fields where they are more sandy. Both Mitcheldean and Littledean lie in a valley of soft, easily eroded red clay. The two villages lie on slightly rising ground in this valley. This valley afforded a passage or route from south to north in pre-Roman and Roman times and the Old Dean Road or Roman Road which was used to carry iron ore north to Ariconium (Weston-under-Penyard) is along this route. Such was the importance of the valley that the old name of valley, 'Dene', gave the name to the Forest.

These Old Red Sandstone rocks formed 350 million years ago now nestle under the younger rocks of the Forest of Dean and hold them as in a cup.

The Quartz Conglomerate

Towards the end of the time of deposition of the Old Red Sandstone

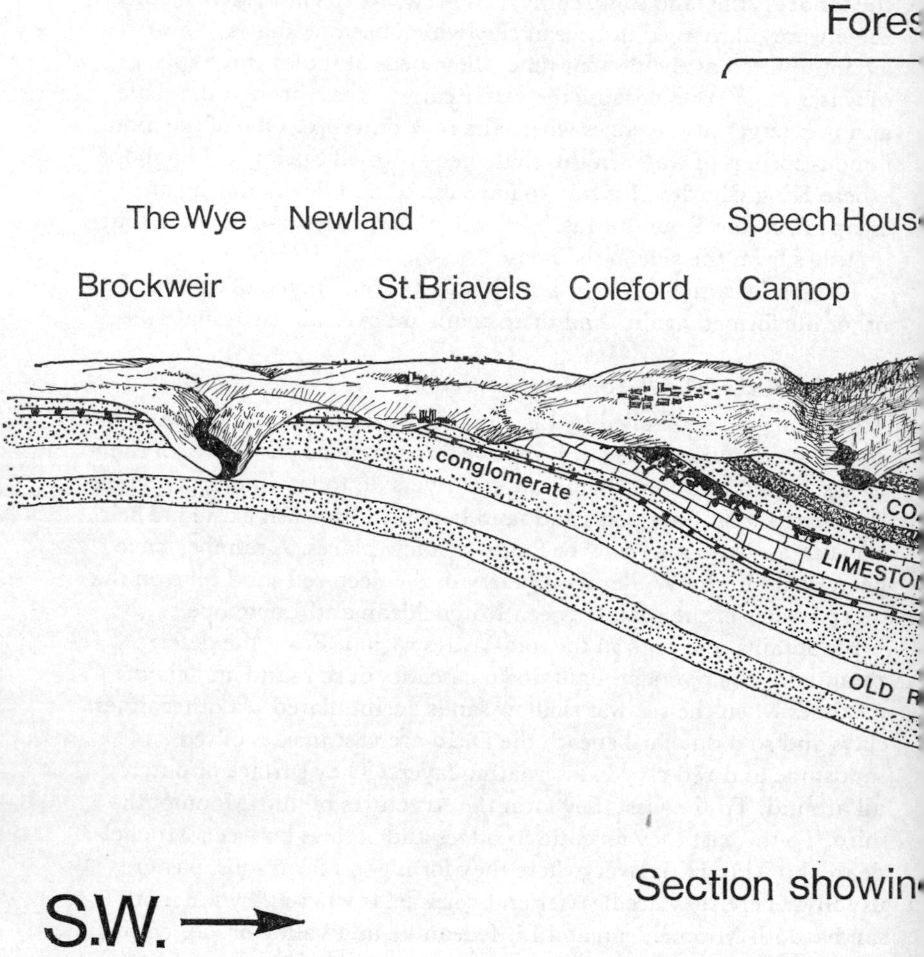

Fores

The Wye   Newland   Speech Hous

Brockweir   St.Briavels   Coleford   Cannop

conglomerate

CO

LIMESTON

OLD R

S.W. →

Section showin

Dean

Cinderford

Drybrook   Edgehills   Lea   May Hill

Mitcheldean Longhope

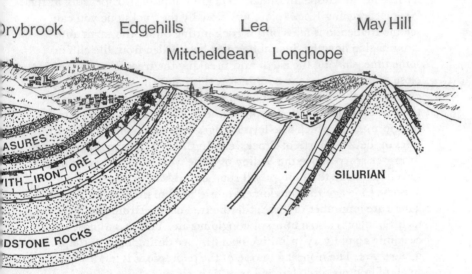

...ASURES

...ITH—IRON—ORE

SILURIAN

...DSTONE ROCKS

Rocks in the Dean area

←—N.E.

 Sandstone

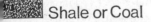 Shale or Coal

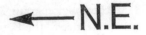 Limestone

mainly Marl

a large river carried pebbles or shingle from the north towards the Dean. This formed a great shingle bank which became solidified into a massive hard rock called 'pudding stone' (because it looks like a currant pudding) or 'conglomerate'. This rock is a very good marker for the geologist. It is, in this region, an indication that one is standing close to the boundary between the Old Red Sandstone rocks and the younger Carboniferous rocks which carry the iron ore and coal seams. Almost all around the edge of the Forest of Dean you will find this conglomerate. A sloping ridge on Coppet Hill (on the right, looking north from Symonds Yat Rock, plates 14 and 15) is caused by it. The Suckstone and Buckstone are lumps of it. Especially at the New Hearkening Rock (plate 57) close by the Suckstone you can see the tremendous mass of this rock jutting out of the earth and can imagine how the Suckstone must have fallen from the cliff at some time, shaking the earth and breaking the trees. You can see in close examination of the boulders at this point the way the changing currents in the delta which deposited this sand and gravel have left their traces. The Naval Temple at the Kymin stands on the same rock formation, which also forms ridges or scarps high up on both sides of the Wye north of Brockweir. In the east the conglomerate forms the scarp above the Valley of Dene where the rocks can be well seen high above the Plump Hill road out of Mitcheldean.

Some time ago the conglomerate was used to make cider presses. There are a number of these still about. The old Drummer Boy Stone near Soudley is also a lump of conglomerate. This was almost certainly an old very primitive iron furnace dating back perhaps 3,000 years. The iron slag in one of the depressions is left from a smelt of iron ore and charcoal mixed together.

To the north the conglomerate outcrops all around the great amphitheatre of Hope Mansel which encloses a dome of Old Red Sandstone. Towards Ross the outlying hills of Penyard are ringed by the conglomerate. At Lea Bailey, the only reasonable northern entrance to the Forest of Dean, the conglomerate stands sentinel on the side of the road guarding the way.

So almost all round the Forest you must cross the conglomerate before you approach the centre. Only at two spots can you avoid this; from the south below Tidenham where younger rocks (The New Red Sandstone) spread over the formation from the east, and north of Lydney where again younger rocks (Carboniferous) spread over it from the centre of the Forest.

Carboniferous Limestones and Drybrook Sandstone

We are still thinking of rocks laid down as sand and shingle by a river delta that existed over 350 million years ago. The delta sank and a quiet warm sea invaded the land. A warm sea such as one may see today by East Africa. Limestones again were formed with the bodies of the curious sea lilies fossilised in them. A succession of limestones deposited over several million years formed on top of the solidifying conglomerate. Then eventually the land began to rise again, especially in the east and south, and sand and shingles again were laid down. The limestones we call Carboniferous Limestones, and the sandstones above them is Drybrook Sandstone.

The Carboniferous limestone and succeeding sandstone follow the same saucer shape curves of the rocks beneath and, therefore, are found outcropping all around the edge of the Dean just inside the conglomerate. At Lea Bailey, just beyond the sentinel of conglomerate, the road passes between cliffs of the limestones. A glance at the section illustrated will show you how to the west these limestones outcrop at a shallow angle to the surface and cover a much larger area than to the east. The limestones produce good farm soils and if you look at a one-inch map of the Dean, or those inside the covers of this Guide, you will see how between St. Briavels, Bream and Coleford, there are farms which lie on these rocks. To the east the outcrop is so narrow that the effect is not so obvious, but in detail the effect is dramatic if you know the ground. Near Mitcheldean, especially by Wigpool Common, some field boundaries next to the Forest follow exactly the geological boundary between limestone and sandstone. The Limestones are commonly divided in four groups. The Limestone Shales are the earliest, then the hard Lower Dolomite followed by the wide-fissured Crease Limestone (plate 56 and front cover) and the whiter close-grained Whitehead Limestone.

At a very much more recent date in the earth's history, the limestones (especially the Crease) became impregnated with iron deposits. These iron deposits have played a very important role in history of man in the Dean. Without doubt, before the Romans came iron was mined here. At Bream and other places near Coleford the Scowles (plate 49) are romantic vestiges of the Roman and pre-Roman industry. These dark chasms, set in sylvan splendour with light gleaming through the gold and russet beeches of autumn, their grey-green trunks tall as cathedral arches and roots clutching and grasping at the limestone blocks, inspire a mystery in the mind and conjure up images of olden men with tallow candles groping as gnomes for the deep red ochres of the iron ore. The Romans, in part, paved their roads with the old slag or cinders from their iron furnaces. This they certainly did near Mitcheldean, and the ford paved with such slag at Cinderford gives the name to that town. On through man's history the iron ore mining continued, large mines eventually being sunk in the 19th century. These became uneconomic and most ceased working about 1918. Some few in the west continued until

1945. Visitors can get some impression of these mines at Clearwell Caves, an old mine open to the public at certain holiday times.

The Limestone itself has, much more recently and especially in the twenty years since 1950, been ground up for road metal and enormous quarries have developed. Perhaps as the nearby motorways are completed this activity will be much reduced. The most favoured material for these quarries is the hard central mass of the limestone called Lower Dolomite. Good exposures are seen in Shakemantle Quarry near Cinderford, along the Wye below Tintern at the Wind Cliff (plate 28) or on Plump Hill near Mitcheldean.

The Drybrook Sandstone which overlies the Carboniferous limestones, produces in great contrast to them, the most acidic soils in the whole district. The vegetation growing over it is naturally heathy and poor with whortleberry, heather and gorse. Poor's Allotment, a Nature Reserve near Tidenham, is partly on this material. The grey-black soil with many sparkling quartz grains indicates this rock beneath.

The Drybrook Sandstone has within its strata, however, some curious variations. Here and there are shaly beds almost verging on coal which suggest that when deposited the land was close by, with muddy shores rich in vegetation. To the west there is a band of limestone within the sandstone presumably laid down in clearer seas further away from the old land mass. This limestone is seen at Wintour's Leap and is 300 feet thick at that place.

On Poor's Allotment the juxtaposition of the two rocks, Drybrook Limestone and Drybrook Sandstone, gives a remarkable change of vegetation type in a short distance.

The Coal Measures: Earth Movements

When the Drybrook Sandstone had been formed some 300 million years ago, there followed a time when this sea bed became uplifted and the rocks were compressed so that they were curved up towards the east and south. Mountains were formed across the area which is now Devon and Somerset, and the whole area became dry land.

Erosion of this land followed until again it was a shallow sea with muddy shores and sand banks. Fresh rocks began to be deposited and they were laid down on the top of the old eroded surface of the Carboniferous limestones and earlier rocks. This is why they overlap the older rocks and spill out of the central area of the Dean, especially north of Lydney. These newly formed rocks are the Coal Measures.

On the ancient muddy shores thick steamy forests grew and their remains formed the coal seams. Quite frequently the forests were buried by the sea and thick beds of sandstones from large rivers to the north and east were deposited on them. Today we see these thick

74

sandstones within the Forest as the Pennant sandstones as at the Bixhead Quarries or along the road near Nailsbridge. These sandstones rise high behind Ruardean to give the highest point in the Forest of Dean of 951 feet.

These coal measures (coal seams and Pennant sandstones) today show most clearly the concentric outcrops within the Forest of Dean. The high land west of the Cannop valley continues to the north, cut by a valley at Upper Lydbrook, and then continues eastwards as the high hills of Ruardean Hill and Ruardean Woodside. Another valley intersects at Drybrook and then the high land turns south passing through Cinderford down towards Staple Edge. The Pennant sandstone which forms this high land also extends north west in a limb towards Symonds Yat and also slightly east towards Wigpool.

The major collection of coal seams outcrop in a circular fashion within this high land and as they erode easily, have formed the very obvious valleys of Cannop and Cinderford and that which includes the Monmouth-Gloucester road. You must not, however, be deceived by the steeply-sided valley continuing below Cinderford through Ruspidge. This is an interesting curiosity but its history is related to more recent geological accidents.

The Cannop-Cinderford valley form a horseshoe around the central highlands of the Supra-Pennant sandstones which are surmounted by Speech House.

Coal Seams

Besides the massed coal seams of the valleys, several others are important. A seam (The Trenchard) close to the edge of the Coal Measures is mined by open-cast working at Howle Hill north of Ruardean. This seam and associated sandstone and shale in that area lies on top of the earliest Carboniferous Limestone (Limestone Shales). In other words, at the time of the great uplift of land at the end of the Drybrook Sandstone deposition a great mass of rock was removed by erosion before this Trenchard seam could be laid down on the new muddy shore. In fact, over 800 feet of sediments must have gone during that time, carried by rivers to form younger deposits in South Wales. This part of the Trenchard seam is now isolated from the rest of it beneath the Dean by the valley north of Ruardean.

Another seam of much greater importance is the Coleford High Delf. This irregularly outcrops all around the Forest and for a great distance its occurrence is very close to the borders of the Dean Forest proper. Inside and above it the sandstones and shales make very poor soils and these are the soils left uncultivated from the very early days of man's settlement. The Coleford High Delf itself is a thick seam of good coal and the free miners and later the deep mines have

extensively worked it. The seam outcrops through the centre of
Cinderford beneath the bus station. The major industrial settlements
of the Dean lie close to this outcrop which is coincidentally close to the
iron and the Forest edge, and at Cinderford, the largest of all these
settlements, all the outcrops are closest to each other.

In the centre of the Forest the Worgreen seam lies close to Speech
House. It is the youngest seam of all and is close enough to the
surface to be worked by open-cast mining. Not far away open-cast
mining has recently been operating in the valley seams near Cinderford. These open cast mines, however, tend to be more productive of
fireclay than coal. Beneath the seams there is frequently a bed clay of
such quality that it makes excellent material for lining furnaces. The
clay is also a curse to the free miners since it makes the floors of the
galleries very sticky and also oozes up so that the galleries get smaller
by this pressure from below.

The Pennant Sandstone massively outcropping between the seams
has also extensively been quarried for building stone, many of the
cottages consisting of this material, as well as many finer buildings
in other parts of the country.

Late Carboniferous Earth Movements

The story of the stones does not at this point end. These rocks so far
described were deposited up to 250 million years ago. The youngest
being those close to Speech House. Again at this time earth movements occurred and all were uplifted, mountains formed and the seas
retreated. The shape of the rocks took on their present form. Acid
waters percolated down from the coal beds and sandstones lying on
top and could have carried the iron from the sands down to the
underlying Crease limestones. Here the waters were neutralised and
the iron was deposited for man later to find.

The last 200 million years

Gradually the mountains were again worn down and the sea came
back. But for many millions of years Wales stayed above the sea.
Young rocks (the New Red Sandstones and marls) were laid over the
Dean. Again the land rose and sank again, through the periods of
deposition of the Cotswold rock (Jurassic) and the White Chalk
(Cretaceous), and the present-day erosion pattern began to emerge.
The rocks of the New Red Sandstone and later periods were stripped
away, leaving just some lapping against the southern area of Dean
south of Tidenham Chase and against the eastern edge of May Hill.
You may see these rocks well as you look over across the Severn
Bridge to the cliffs at Aust or if you go to Westbury Garden Cliff.
At both places the curious and characteristic red and 'tea green'

Plate 37. Paddling

Plate 40. Douglas fir

marls are seen. As you look across the river towards the Cotswolds a little imagination only is needed to see how they also could have once reached over to the Dean.

Recent erosion

Now the history is nearly at an end, but not quite. The present land shape is mostly determined by the action of the rivers and the climate of fairly recent times playing on the rocks beneath. During the Ice Ages of up to 2 million years ago, the Dean remained relatively free of ice, though it seems that an ice-cap was on the top for some time. Certainly the deep freezing and thawing, that repeatedly continued, have given rise to some curiously compacted soils in the Dean, making them very difficult to work; here and there are thick masses of a silty clay caused by the same action. This clay is especially marked on the slopes of the Cannop and Cinderford valleys and in the centre of Wigpool. During these glacial times streams flowed torrentially at times of thaw and cut steep channels in the hillsides. This is, no doubt, how the steep gullies at Plump Hill (Mitcheldean), Upper Lydbrook and perhaps part of the Ruspidge valley were formed.

Problems of the rivers

This leaves us with two geological problems, the formation of the River Wye, and the Ruspidge to Blakeney Brook. Both are probably related to the same causes. The problem of the River Wye can be immediately appreciated by a visit to Symonds Yat Rock. There, look north and you see a fairly low-lying landscape (plates 14 and 15). The river flows from this plain, meandering in and out of sight in front of you. It continues south between hills and cliffs to the River Severn. How does it happen that a river takes such a difficult course from low land into high hills cutting across hard and soft rocks in apparently a quite indiscriminate fashion?

The only answer that has been satisfactorily put forward is that the River Wye is very ancient and began to flow long before the Ice Ages, long before the younger rocks of the Chalk and Cotswolds were denuded to their present levels. Indeed, as we have seen, some of these rocks probably existed over the Dean. The river matured and wore these rocks down and slowly meandered across a level plain. The land continued to rise (or the sea sink) and the river cut down to the rocks beneath, and etched itself in.

Occasionally, a meander was nipped by erosion and isolated. This will conceivably happen at Symonds Yat if the rock erodes away. Signs of ancient cut-off meanders like this occur around the Chase and Penyard hills (meeting again at Ross), at Newland where the valleys

77

from Upper and Lower Redbrook are the remains of it, and also in front of St. Briavels Castle.

The other much smaller stream at Ruspidge and Blakeney, though rising within the Dean, also cuts across all the rocks of the area in turn, displaying a curious zig-zag route. For stretches the brook follows the rocks and then at intervals it cuts in a deep cleft across them. This river course is the result of a complex history of erosion but it leaves for us today a beautiful wooded valley which even the worst activities of the Dean's industrial history has not irreparably destroyed. The works of man are recent, no more than 2,000 years, and for the most part of no great consequence but for those of the last 200 years. He is here holding in trust a history of 400 million years. The rocks themselves speak to us and make us humble.

In Devil's Chapel they dug the ore
Two thousand years ago and more,
Earth's veins of gleaming metal showing
Like crusted blood first set a-glowing
Phoenician faces.

Devil's Chapel   F.W.Harvey

Free miners

Readers who wish to follow up in detail the geology of the Forest can do no better than read *Geology Explained in the Forest of Dean and Wye Valley* by W.Dreghorn. That author gives a further good bibliography.

A Drive Round the Forest of Dean

Herbert L. Edlin

The tour outlined below has been planned to include all the outstanding features of the Dean Forest. In the main it follows the rim
of high hills that almost encircles the Forest, and provides amazing
views over Herefordshire to the north, and Gloucestershire and the
Severn on the east and south. But between Blakeney and Lydney it
plunges deep into the Forest's heart, along winding valleys em-
bowered in oaks, to reach the Speech House and the Cannop Ponds.

The total length is some 50 miles, and though it could be covered
in a few hours, it demands a whole day if halts are made to visit the
more fascinating woods and antiquities. Because it seeks the hills, it
cannot be easy going for the cyclist, and there are three "unrideable"
climbs. Again, though many of the roads are bus routes, they do not
make a pattern that would help the walker.

For convenience, it is assumed that the tourist starts at the Camp
Site. As this is a circular tour, it could alternatively begin and end
at several points, including Coleford, Cinderford, Mitcheldean,
Newnham, Littledean, the Speech House, and Lydney. Those who
come from Gloucester should join and leave the circle at Elton, by
following the Chepstow road A48 towards Newnham. (Start at
'Pleasant Stile' below.)

Christchurch (Berry Hill) to Plump Hill and Mitcheldean

The road from the Camp Site leads to the Christchurch crossroads
(marked 'Berry Hill' on the Ordnance Map). Proceed across them
to follow the road signposted 'Five Acres'. At the next crossroads
(compulsory halt again) turn left on to the main Monmouth–
Gloucester road (A4136) which you will follow (except for possible
diversions) for the next eight miles.

You travel now along a high ridge, 700 feet above sea level, between the Wye and the Severn valleys. There are broad screens of
beech trees, which also serve as fire belts, on either side of the road,
with extensive plantations of young conifers beyond them. At Edge
End, where there is a picnic site (Carters Green) a grand view
towards the north, over the plain of Hereford, opens out on your left.
Thence the road drops, again between woodlands, towards Upper
Lydbrook. On the right you can see the Serridge fire lookout tower,
which stands on an old colliery tip, now completely screened by
pinewoods. After the Lydbrook cross-roads, the road climbs to the
hamlet of Brierley.

Diversion to Ruardean Hill. Take the second left turn at Brierley and bear right repeatedly to gain the summit of Ruardean Hill, 951 feet above sea level and the highest point in the Forest. It commands wonderful views over Herefordshire towards May Hill and the Malvern Hills on the north. Continue to bear right until you rejoin the main road (A4136) and turn left on to it to resume the main tour.

Main Route

Continuing by the main road, you will soon see tall woods of Norway spruce on your right, while to the left, set back a little, are extensive coppice crops of sweet chestnut, grown to provide small poles and pulpwood. Soon you will pass, on your right, the Northern Colliery, which was the last big one to remain active in the Dean; until 1965 over 2,000 tons of coal were raised there every week. The road falls to the Nailbridge cross roads, and you will see ahead, on a knoll, the prominent Forest Church.

NOTE. A right turn at Nailbridge leads into Cinderford, 2 miles away. It is the largest town in the Forest, but its industries hold little attraction for the tourist.

Our main route winds uphill from Nailbridge, until an electric cable overhead marks the summit of Plump Hill, 780 feet. Now an immense prospect opens out on your right, over the Vale of Gloucester and the bends of the Severn towards the long ridge of the Cotswold Hills. To enjoy it, draw off the road on to one of the greens, grazed by the wandering sheep, amid the scattered, picturesque cottages. (Plate 51).

Mitcheldean, Flaxley Valley, The Severn Shore and Newnham (plate 20)

Proceed carefully down the long hill into Mitcheldean, where the road forks. Take the right fork, and immediately (at the same road junction) a right turn signposted 'Flaxley Abbey'. This passes the large modern Abenhall County Secondary School and then follows a long valley south, below Plump Hill. The old Abenhall Church lies on your left, and beyond the first junction, where you keep left, the prehistoric fort of Welshbury stands on its hill top. The road now winds through a beautiful pastoral valley, set between the Flaxley Woods (left) and the Welshbury Woods (right) (plate 21). Soon you see, on the left, Flaxley Abbey, once the home of a religious community but now a private mansion, set in a lovely park, with a church close by. At Flaxley School bear right, and keep straight on through fields and orchards to the main road at Elton. Here you turn right, on to the main Gloucester-Chepstow road (A48), following a signpost to 'Chepstow'.

Follow this high road for two miles into Newnham; for nearly a mile it hugs the bank of the Severn. If the water is low you will see the sandbanks; if it is high you may watch the smooth flow of its tides.

If a spring tide is running up, you may be lucky enough to witness the famous Severn bore, a series of tidal waves when the incoming tide reverses the current.

Pleasant Stile Hill, Littledean and Abbotswood Plantations

Newnham is a pleasing town with a tree-lined main street and some well-designed old houses. In its centre stands a prominent clock tower, and after you pass this you will see, on the right, a side-road signposted 'Pleasant Stile'. Take this right turn and climb by a steep winding road through grassy fields to the summit of Dean Hill. Halt here and look over the wall on the right for another grand prospect of the Severn levels and the distant city of Gloucester.

Proceeding, drop steeply down into Littledean. Turn left (after halting) and then after 100 yards, sharp left again, on to a by-road signposted 'Soudley'. This descends through fields to Abbotswood. Shortly after you meet the trees again, look out for two large ponds on the left; these are the upper Soudley ponds. There is room to park where a forest road (not open to cars) runs in between them.

Take a stroll here to see the remarkable range of forest plots, where trees of many kinds are grown in different ways so that rates of growth, and methods of tending, can be compared. Some lie along the public road, whilst others border the forest roads to right and left, on the far side of the ponds. The Douglas firs to the right of the public road are particularly fine.

Down the Soudley Valley to Blakeney (plate 13)

Now drive on down the hill, through more plantations, to Soudley, and turn left. A little further on you will see, on your left, the lowest of the Soudley ponds, fringed by thriving Douglas fir. A camping ground for Boy Scouts lies close by. From this point on you follow the only road down the delightful Soudley valley, past woods, pastures and cottages above a meandering brook, until you reach the main road (A48) at Blakeney.

Blakeney to the Roman Road and the Speech House (plate 5)

At Blakeney, turn right on to the high road (signposted "Chepstow") and after only 300 yards leave it by another right turn on to a road signposted 'Coleford' and 'The Barracks'. This runs up a valley between fields and cottages, for half a mile, and then plunges deep into the oakwoods of the Blakeney Walk. About one mile farther on, you will see on your right a turning signposted 'Soudley', at a corner where there is space to park. Leave your car, follow the by-road under a disused railway bridge, and you will find, a hundred yards further on, a short stretch of an ancient Roman road. This

81

was built in the first or second century A.D., between Lydney and Mitcheldean, and its course has been traced for 10½ miles.

Now go on by the principal road which winds up a valley below the steep slopes of Staple Edge to emerge on a hill top close to The Barracks, which will be seen on the right. These rows of terrace houses were originally built for miners at the old 'New Fancy' colliery nearby, but are now occupied by forest workers. Just past them, take a right turn signposted 'Speech House'. The road now runs between two huge mine tips, locally called "tumps"; that on the right has been burnt out, and its red shale is being steadily carted away for foundation material; that on the left, which is unburnt and therefore still black, is being screened by tree planting. A long stretch of level woodland follows, until the imposing Speech House itself appears on the right.

Speech House to Cannop Ponds and Parkend (plate 22)

The Speech House, built by Charles II in 1680, is the old centre of the Forest's administration, and the Verderers Court still meets here. It is now an hotel, but the courtroom, now used as a dining hall, may be seen by the public at any reasonable hour.

If you wish to visit the Arboretum, a collection of rare specimen trees that is open to the public, turn right at the road junction, proceed to the end of a field, park your car, and then take a forest track that strikes off to the right just beyond the field.

Otherwise, turn left, signposted 'Coleford' and carefully descend the very steep hill (1 in 6), with its misleading bends, to Cannop Cross roads. Here, turn left (signposted 'Lydney'). Soon you will see, on your left, the mile-long stretch of the Cannop Ponds. These are fringed with oak and beech, and are well stocked with coarse fish and ornamental water fowl. Just beyond them, a stone dressing mill makes use of locally quarried material. Next you near Parkend, and enter it by turning right and proceeding over a level crossing.

Diversion to Shorten the Tour. By bearing right a second time in Parkend, you will join the road leading to Coleford and, by omitting Lydney, shorten the tour by ten miles.

Down the Lydney Valley

To follow the main route, turn left at Parkend (signposted 'Lydney'). Beyond a level crossing, the road follows the charming wooded valley of the little Cannop Brook, also called the River Lyd. Parkhill Enclosure, with its grand beeches and Douglas firs, is seen on the right, and may be entered, on foot, through one of several gateways.

At Whitecroft, where there is a large factory making pins, bear left, then right, to follow the valley downstream. The larches of the

Kidnalls Woods rise towards Yorkley on the left, while to the right the Old Park Woods, which are privately owned as part of the Lydney Park estate, clothe the steep slopes. The road, now deep in a wooded gorge, continues its tortuous course into Lydney, a small industrial town and river port

The hills of Bream

At Lydney, turn right (signposted 'Chepstow') on to the main A48 road, go over a level crossing, and almost at once take another right turn, signposted 'Bream'. This climbs steadily up a ridge, giving good views to the right over the woodlands of the Lyd valley, which you have recently traversed. Soon it enters the Old Park Woods, and you may note, on the right, a small coal mine or 'gale', opened by a group of Free Miners. The famous Scowles, where iron ore was dug in Roman times, lie in the Lydney Park woods on the left, near their northern end.

Bear right as you enter Bream, and halt for a moment at the prominent war memorial. It gives a breathtaking view over the heart of the Dean Forest, with nothing ahead for miles save a green sea of trees..

From Bream past Parkend to Coleford

The descent through Bream towards Parkend runs at first through a council estate, but soon the sylvan woods are regained. A feature of interest here is the rapid colonisation of abandoned spoil heaps and stone quarries by birch, alder, willow, and similar fast growing broadleaved trees. At the hill foot, by an old toll house with a 'give way' sign, turn sharp left to leave Parkend by the Coleford road.

The road winds on up a long valley, through oakwoods open to grazing sheep and past stone quarries and small coal mines. At Coalway it gains a ridge top, parting Severn from Wye. Go straight on over the cross-roads, to descend a hill that gives a good view of Coleford, an old country town with a grammar school, church, market square, and some modern factories. At the hill foot, bear left for the clocktower at its centre. There turn right, then shortly after right again, to climb a hill to the New Inn cross-roads. Go on across these to the Christchurch (Berry Hill) cross-roads that were your starting point.

The Road to Ross, May Hill and Huntley

Christchurch to Ross

No visitor to the Camp Site should miss the fine scenery of the by-road into Ross-on-Wye, ten miles away; it is an easy run by car, and there is also a bus service (Red-and-White no. 35). The road starts just beside the church, and leads first to English Bicknor, giving grand views west over Herefordshire on the way. It then drops down a beautiful valley, first between fields, then through young woodlands, to Lower Lydbrook. Just across the river stands Welsh Bicknor; although this is actually in Herefordshire, not Wales, it retained its name because Welsh manorial customs were long observed there, in contrast to English customs in the twin manor of English Bicknor in Gloucestershire.

Lydbrook is a straggling village that once mined coal and made steel cables. Its factories now produce cardboard packages, light engineering goods and house extension materials.

The road now winds through a picturesque gorge cut by the Wye, with the young plantations of Thomas Wood on the farther bank. At Kerne Bridge you may cross the river (there is now no toll) for Goodrich village and Goodrich Castle. If you keep straight on, you will gain a grand view of the Castle, standing boldly on a bluff above the stream. Then the road runs on through Walford, and below the thickly wooded slopes of Chase Wood and Penyard Park—both outliers of the Dean Forest, into Ross town.

Ross to May Hill and Huntley

At Ross-on-Wye, do not fail to see the fine sweep of the river just north of the main street, and close to the Hereford road. To see a fresh aspect of the Dean's varied scenery, leave the town by the main Gloucester road, A40 (Ross–Gloucester bus route). This runs through fertile land where apples, plums and cherries are grown in thriving orchards that become a sea of blossom every spring. Near Weston-under-Penyard, the bold bluff of the Penyard Park Woods, now a part of the Dean Forest, rises nobly to the south. Farther on, near Lea village, you see the still higher tree-clad slopes of Wigpool Common, which rise to 900 feet and have always formed part of the Dean.

May Hill now comes plainly into view on the left, its sweep of bracken-clad common land topped by a clump of pines. It is 971 feet high, and thus exceeds any hill in the Dean, and it is owned by the National Trust. At Dursley Cross, at the top of a long winding hill, you can turn off left along a by-road to a point below its summit, which is gained by a short steep path. The view includes the Lower Severn valley, the Cotswolds, the Malvern Hills, and the plain of Hereford.

The main Gloucester road, beyond Dursley Cross, drops down Huntley Hill through the well-tended woods of the Huntley Manor estate. These woods were formerly owned by the late Major C. P. Ackers, a pioneer of modern scientific forestry on private estates in Britain, who wrote a leading textbook and became President of the Royal Forestry Society of England, Wales, and Northern Ireland.

View west over Lea Village, towards Penyard and Ross, from the Gloucester Road

He also founded a firm, Forest Products Ltd., which operates extensive nursery gardens and a big sawmill at Huntley.

Huntley to Christchurch

From Huntley village you may go on, if you wish, to Gloucester, now only 7½ miles ahead. The shortest return route to the Camp Site is by the Gloucester-Monmouth road, A4136 reached by a right turn at the Huntley sawmill. This runs first through orchards and past wood turneries into the Longhope valley, then climbs Brimps Hill for Mitcheldean. Next it winds up the steep Plump Hill, with its fine views, to enter the Dean Forest and run right across its northern heights to Five Acres, where a right turn leads to Christchurch.

Therefore am I still
A lover of the meadows and the woods,
And mountains, and of all that we behold
From this green earth.

Wordsworth

A Tour of the Wye Valley Woodlands

Herbert L. Edlin

The tour described below brings in the best of the forest scenery of the lower Wye Valley and the Forest of Dean. Its total length is about fifty miles.

For convenience, it is assumed that the visitor makes it by car—it *could* be so done in an afternoon, but it would be far better to devote a whole day to it, so as to spend a fair spell of time at several of the many vantage points. A cyclist should allow a whole day, though there is only one major hill—that between Huntsham Bridge and Symonds Yat Rock.

Chepstow has been chosen as a convenient, well-known, starting point. But one could join this circular tour at convenient intermediate points such as Tintern, Monmouth, Symonds Yat, the Christchurch Camp Site, Coleford or the Severn Bridge.

Leave Chepstow by Welsh Street, just above the archway across the High Street, and follow the main road (A466) signposted *Monmouth*. Bear right at the roundabout and note, on the hill slope to the left, the trees of Frith Wood, an outlying portion of Chepstow Forest. Pass the Chepstow Racecourse and bear right at the village of St. Arvans.

The Wind Cliff

After St. Arvans and before the main road enters the forest at a series of bends, a minor road to the left, signposted 'Wyndcliffe', leads to the Upper Wind Cliff car park. From here, itself an excellent view point, there is a nature trail which includes visiting a look-out and view point perched on top of the wooded cliff, with extensive views over the Lower Wye Gorge and the Severn estuary.

Following the main road from St. Arvans to Tintern, shortly after entering the forest, there are wooded parking areas at the Lower Wind Cliff. From the car park on the lower side of the road short paths lead to viewpoints overlooking the Wye. From the car park above the road a path leads to the 365-step footpath climbing the cliffs to the look-out and viewpoint. This link path enables the active people in a party to travel on foot, leaving a driver to move the car between upper and lower car parks if desired.

Tintern Abbey

Continuing along the main road, you pass the fields of Liveoaks Farm, and then go through the woods below Black Cliff, which include some fine native lime trees. Soon Tintern Abbey springs into view on the right, and most people will wish to halt close beside it, where there are car parks, hotels and restaurants, to see the picturesque ruins. Go down to the river bank and you will find that, though the sea is far out of sight, the Wye is still tidal here. The woods on the steep slopes beyond it form part of Tidenham Chase; those on the nearer side lie within Tintern Forest.

White Stone Plantations

Go on by the main road through Tintern Village, till you reach the prominent Wye Valley Hotel. Here strike left up a narrow pastoral valley dotted with cottages. Soon the Tintern woods close in on both sides, and after keeping right at a junction, you reach a crossroads marked by a prominent white upright stone. Halt here to see the varied examples of forest crops.

Above the road, exceptionally fine European larches, planted by the Duke of Beaufort in 1879, tower above a lower canopy of beech. In the triangle just behind the White Stone itself, trees of many kinds are springing up in a clearing, arising from seeds that the winds and birds have carried in; they include larch, beech, oak, wild cherry, Douglas fir, ash, and Western red cedar.

Walk down the road signposted "Llandogo" to see, on the right, the grandest larches in all this forest; growing amid beech, they were planted in 1850 and are now over 100 feet tall. On your way back to the White Stone, note on the hill, a fine stand of Norway spruce, planted in 1913, which has already been thinned out several times; the attractive roadside trees, however, are Western red cedars.

Llandogo to Monmouth

Leave the White Stone by the road signposted 'Llandogo'. Dropping down between larches on your left and Douglas firs on your right, you soon enjoy a wide view across the Wye valley towards St. Briavels Church, a landmark on the far hill. When you rejoin the main road at Llandogo, turn left for Monmouth. Soon the Tintern woods come down again on the left, and the main road swings right to cross the Wye by Bigsweir Bridge, the highest point to which tides flow.

Over the bridge, the road enters Gloucestershire and bears left. For the next three miles it follows a lovely, lonely, wooded defile. The Hael Woods along the farther, Monmouthshire, bank form part of Tintern Forest. Those woods that come down to the roadside on the right are being developed and replanted by a group of private owners. At Redbrook the road, though still keeping to the eastern bank, re-enters Monmouthshire. The woods now in view on the left, and on the hills that lie ahead, are all in Tintern Forest. Soon the old town of Monmouth itself is reached, by a bridge over the Wye, and those who wish to explore it, and to see the famous gate-house on the bridge over the Monnow (plate 35), are advised to halt and park their cars in the signposted park.

Monmouth to Symonds Yat Rock

Leave Monmouth by the Ross road (A40); this was recently developed to form a part of the main trunk road from Birmingham, via Ross, to Swansea. It soon runs close beside the Wye with the Hayes Coppice woods of Tintern Forest rising on the left. Where the road crosses the Herefordshire boundary, the thriving plantations of a private estate, Wyaston Leys, may be seen rising prominently up the limestone hill called Little Doward (724 feet). Beyond this point, the fertile plain of Herefordshire opens out, with the long rocky ridge of Coppet Hill towards the right, and one reaches the picturesque village of Whitchurch.

Diversion to Symonds Yat West. From Whitchurch a by-road, leading only to Symonds Yat West, diverges to the left. It runs for 1½miles to the village, where there are hotels, cafes, boats and a ferry over the Wye (plate 6). It provides a good approach to Lord's Wood, a Forestry Commission property on the steep limestone slopes of Great Doward Hill.

Continuing the main route for Symonds Yat Rock, diverge left from the main Ross road, one mile beyond Whitchurch, taking a side-road (B4429) signposted 'Goodrich'. After proceeding for a further mile, you will see, on the right hand, a by-road signposted 'Symonds Yat Rock and Coleford'. Turn down this, and you will shortly cross the Wye by the slender Huntsham Bridge; from this point our route runs southwards.

Diversion to Symonds Yat East. One mile beyond the bridge, a road bears right for Symonds Yat East, but it is very narrow and has only one turning bay; the only parking places are those owned by hotels.

Main route resumed

To gain Symonds Yat Rock, keep left-handed up th narrow road that runs up the very steep limestone slopes. At the summit, you pass below a wooden footbridge and see, immediately on your right, the entrance to the Forestry Commission car park. There is a remarkable refreshment pavilion here, built by the forest staff in 1956, using local grown logs of Western red cedar on the log-cabin principle which is traditional in Norway, Switzerland and North America, but rarely seen in England. They used 78 logs, holding 287 cubic feet of timber, and made 134 notched joints. Shingles of the same very durable timber, imported from Canada, were used for the roof; while cedar planking was also used to build the public conveniences nearby. (Plate 10).

Views from the Yat Rock

Leave your car and cross the wooden footbridge. Take a few steps along the rocky path, bear right and gaze right-handed and you will see the Wye sweeping below the limestone crags on its way down from Hereford and Ross. Follow its course with your gaze, now straight ahead, and you will see it running north in a great loop back towards Goodrich spire between Coppet Hill and Huntsham Hill, as shown in our pictures. Look left-handed, and you will find it returning to glide below the cottages of Symonds Yat, on the wooded Great Doward Hill.

Retrace your steps to the pavilion for a clearer view of the Symonds Yat gorge, now directly below you. It is just possible to see, round to your left, the last of the *four* stretches of this meandering stream where it plunges between Lord's Wood and The Slaughter on its way towards Monmouth and the sea. A better view can be gained by following adventurous footpaths left-handed till you gain the Lion Rock, just above the Wye Rapids. Care is needed everywhere along these viewpoints, as they are unfenced, with sheer precipices below (plates 14 and 15).

Symonds Yat Rock to Coleford

Back in the car, turn right when you come on to the public road (B4432). You are now on a high ridge, some 600 feet above sea level, between the Wye and the Severn, and you will follow it all the way south to Chepstow. On the right, the plantations of the High-meadow Woods run continuously for two miles. Where they end, you pass a public picnic ground, and enter the village of Christchurch, marked by its church and large garage. Here turn right, following, *but only at first*, signs to 'Monmouth'.

Diversion to Camping Ground. Within Christchurch village, a by-road clearly signposted, leads to the main Camping Ground of the Dean Forest Park.
(*Main route resumed*)
A mile beyond Christchurch, on the 'Monmouth' road, you reach a cross-roads called 'New Inn'. Here go straight on, down a hill, and bear left for the main square of the picturesque market town of Coleford (plate 7). Dead ahead, you will see a prominent clock tower, and the Chepstow road (B4228), which you are to follow, runs on just behind this.

Coleford to Chepstow

Climbing out of Coleford, you reach, after 1½ miles, the fringe of the real Forest of Dean. At Clearwell Meend you will find the road unfenced, with sheep grazing peacefully below ancient oaks. Soon fields close in again, and after passing Orepool Inn and Trow

Green, you skirt the young woods of Bearse Common, part of Tidenham Chase.

St. Briavel's village (pronounced Saint Brevvel's) merits a halt because of its well-chosen situation on a hill-top that gives wide views west over the Wye. Its castle is now a Youth Hostel, and though it is not open to the public you can walk, or even drive, round the circular moat that encloses it; it was for long the centre of the Forest administration, as well as a bulwark against Welsh invaders. The old church stands hard by.

Our Chepstow road now runs south towards the main block of Tidenham Chase, through which it winds for nearly a mile. When it emerges again into open fields, a magnificent view of the Severn, with the Vale of Berkeley and the Cotswold Hills beyond, is revealed; prominent in the picture are the Sharpness Docks, Berkeley Castle, and the new atomic power station at Oldbury-on-Severn.

Two views of the Lower Wye Gorge

Soon the road falls sharply, and, just after a side-road has come in on the left, you will see on the right a curious 'chair' cut in a yew hedge. Just beyond this, a short path on the right leads to a surprising view west across the Wye to the woods of Tintern.

Beyond a by-road on the right, signposted 'Lancaut only' a winding stretch of road follows. After it straightens out, go on for 200 yards, and you will then approach a second, distant, viewpoint— the famous Wintour's Leap. It is not at present marked by any sign, but a widening of the roadway makes it possible to leave a car. Neither of these two views is visible from the road itself, although the road comes within a few yards of their sheer drops.

The road continues on towards Chepstow, two miles away. Bear right at the first fork, then right at the next junction, and descend the steep, winding slope to Chepstow Bridge. This is a slender iron structure which has carried remarkably heavy traffic—up to 24 tons

View from Lydbrook over the Wye towards Welsh Bicknor and the Black Mountains

90

Building Severn trows with Dean oak at Chepstow, about 1896

in weight, ever since it was built in 1816. To the left, limestone cliffs
spring sheer from the tidal river, while to the right, the full sweep of the
Chepstow Castle walls are seen (plate 26). Over the bridge, and the
route runs up the busy streets of the town, past the old Church with
its Norman west front, to the archway that was our starting point.

Around Chepstow

Very attractive views of wooded limestone valleys and sandstone
hilltops can be seen in a short, fourteen-mile round tour from
Chepstow. Go along Welsh Street and continue to the roundabout.
There you take the left turn signposted 'Newport', but only 100
yards farther on turn off right for 'Usk'. Almost at once you find
yourself running between the young plantations of the Great
Barnets Woods; beech is seen on the right, while on the left a variety
of coniferous trees, and some beech, have been planted below a
screen of less valuable hardwoods.

Next you cross a strip of fields, and see ahead a *very sharp* right-
handed bend, marked by an arrow. If you care to halt a good
hundred yards back from this bend, you will find, on the left, a footpath that affords, a short way down, a fine view of the lower
Mounton valley, with its sheer limestone rocks topped by old
beeches, ash trees and yews. The trees, shrubs, and plants hereabouts
are all characteristic of the limestone—you will see dogwood,
spindle tree, field maple, and traveller's joy. A remarkable rarity
is the wild service tree, *Sorbus torminalis*, which has bark like a
hawthorn, leaves like a maple, flowers like a rowan tree, and brown-
ish-red berries that taste like a pear!

Proceeding along the Usk road, you follow the winding course of
the Mounton Brook, fringed by pastures, below hillside plantations
on either hand. As you climb to the scattered village of Mynydd
Bach—a Welsh name meaning the lesser moorland—the view opens

out over rolling pastures. The scattered woods on the steeper slopes all form part of Tintern Forest, and away to the north is seen the broad expanse of the Chepstow Park Woods, which spread for two miles along the hillside.

At the *Cross Hands Inn*, turn right, then bear right, one mile on, for Itton. There you follow a road signposted 'Devauden', to run through the Chepstow Park plantations. These are largely of conifers, mainly Douglas fir and Japanese larch, but many belts of beech and oak have been left as screens and firebreaks.

At Devauden Green, it is a good plan to halt and enjoy the view to the north-west, which ranges as far as the Brecon Beacons. Then turn right, on to the high road towards Chepstow town. This runs between Chepstow Park Wood on the right, and Fedw Wood of Tintern Forest on the left, to Pen y Parc. There it emerges from between the trees and a grand view is obtained over the Lower Severn, extending on a clear day to the Somerset Hills. Thence the road drops steadily to St. Arvans, and you continue straight on to the roundabout and so back into Chepstow.

The sounding cataract
Haunted me like a passion: the tall rock
The mountain, and the deep and gloomy wood,
Their colours and their forms, were then to me
An appetite; a feeling and a love,
That had no need of a remoter charm
By thought supplied.

Wordsworth

Plate 41. Huntsmen and hounds meet at the Speech House

Plate 42. Pathfinders

Plate 43. Elephant hawk-moth, newly emerged

Plate 44. Dragonfly

Plate 45. Damselfly

Plate 46. Comma butterfly

Plate 47. Horshoe bats, hanging upside down from the roof of their cave

Plate 48. Adder: note its characteristic zig-zag back marking

Rambles in Dean Forest and Wye Valley

The Ramblers Association
Gloucestershire and District.
Hon. Secretary: A.J. Drake

"A ramblers' paradise" is a fair description of the Dean Forest and Wye Valley Forest Park, as the Forestry Commission allows the walker to roam almost anywhere in the woodlands under its control. The hilly terrain, the deep gorges of the Wye, the great variety of tree species grown, and the many points of historical interest all help to make walking in the Forest Park a rewarding and pleasurable pastime. Of the twelve rambles described in the ensuing pages, four are almost completely within Forestry Commission woodlands, while the others follow both forest and field routes. The superb scenery of the Lower Wye Valley is seen from nine of the rambles, sometimes from the riverside and at other times from high up on the valley slopes and rocky outcrops.

Maps. It must be emphasised that a map on a scale of not less than one inch to the mile is essential for following the descriptions for Rambles (4) to (11), whether amongst the maze of tracks in the Forest of Dean or on the fieldpaths. For navigation the maps most recommended are the Ordnance Survey, one inch to the mile numbers 142, 143 and 155. The 1 : 25,000 scale maps ($2\frac{1}{2}$ inches to one miles) showing all paths known to the Ordnance Survey, are listed under the separate rambles. Within this Guide, the endpaper maps show the general direction of all the numbered walks described here; but their scale is too small to carry close detail.

Grid references are sometimes used in the descriptions. This is to enable the walker to pin-point his position on the map at difficult points, by reference to the grid lines on Ordnance maps. The references given here are 'Six-Figure' ones; their appropriate prefix is: so.

Caution. Every endeavour has been made to ensure correctness of the detail given for the rambles that follow, but neither the Ramblers Association nor the Forestry Commission accept legal responsibility for the accuracy of the information given.

Access by bus to the area is mostly provided by Red-&-White Services Ltd. the Bulwark, Chepstow, Mon., but there are *no Sunday morning services.*

Waymarked Forest Paths Rambles, 1, 2 and 3

The Forest of Dean and Highmeadow Woods have been the scene of a pioneer waymarking experiment by the Ramblers Association in collaboration with the Forestry Commission. The waymarking system

differs from that normally found in the Alps, Black Forest, etc. in that
it is an "all arrow" system and that it uses yellow paint. An arrow
pointing upwards means go straight on, while one tilting to one side
indicates the deviation to be made, in similar manner to the system
used for advance road signs. Two sets of arrows have been put up,
one for each way along the path, so that the waymarked paths can be
followed in either direction. If you get to a junction with no arrows,
go back to the last arrow you saw because you will almost certainly
have missed one. This may sound too obvious but experience has
shown that those who get lost have usually not done this. Leaflets
about the waymarked paths and points of interest on the routes are
published for the Highmeadow Path (2p) and for the two Forest of
Dean routes (2p), and can be obtained from the Christchurch camp
site, the Log Cabins at Symonds Yat Rock and Speech House or by
post from the Gloucestershire Footpath Secretary of the Ramblers
Association, Mr A. J. Drake, 2 Beech Lodge, The Park, Cheltenham
GL50 2RX (send stamped addressed envelope).

---

1 The Highmeadow Circular Waymarked Forest Path

Distance 10 miles. Allow 6 hours including one hour meal break.

Maps are not essential, but useful is the one-inch-to-one-mile, no. 142,
    and the 1 : 25,000 scale map no. so/51.
    The Highmeadow Path leaflet mentioned above has a sketch
    map 1 : 25,000 scale and shows the main tree compartments.
    Only a brief account is needed as the route is so well indicated.

For river and forest scenery and for general interest this ramble can
have few equals in Britain. Highmeadow Woods are about 3½ miles
wide by 2 miles long and lie between Symonds Yat, Monmouth and
Coleford. The Woods are cut through by one of the most picturesque
sections of the Wye Valley and the waymarked path crosses the river
by the foot suspension bridge at the Biblins, and also by the ferry
near the disused railway station at Symonds Yat. The waymarked
path can be followed in either direction and links up many points of
interest including the breathtaking view from Symonds Yat Rock,
King Arthur's Cave, Seven Sisters Rocks, the Ecological Reserve,
Near Hearkening Rock, Staunton Long Stone, Suckstone and
Buckstone. Useful starting points are Ready Penny Picnic site
(½ mile north of Berry Hill on B4433), the Christchurch camp site,
and Symonds Yat Rock. The route is quite steep and rough in places
but the high level portion from Staunton to Symonds Yat Rock via
Christchurch has little change of level.
    White-arrowed routes cut across the middle of the Highmeadow

Woods from the Christchurch and Braceland camp sites to the river Wye at the Biblins, so that the circuit can be walked in two halves if desired. These routes are shown but not numbered, on endpaper maps.

A one-mile spur route links the Highmeadow circuit at the Buckstone, through Bunjups Wood to the Offa's Dyke Long Distance Path at Upper Redbrook, this too is shown on the endpaper map, but not numbered.

2 St Briavels to Mitcheldean Waymarked Forest Path

Distance 14 miles. Allow about $7\frac{1}{2}$ hours including one hour meal break. The Forest of Dean section from Bream Cross to the Wilderness is $10\frac{1}{2}$ miles. *Maps* O.S. 1-inch sheets 143 and 155.

This route, waymarked by the Ramblers Association in 1960, goes right across the Forest of Dean, and was primarily intended as a walking link between the Youth Hostels at Mitcheldean and St. Briavels. The route was carefully chosen to include a variety of forest scenery such as is probably unsurpassed in Britain. As far as possible the townships on the fringe of the Forest, and industrial disfigurements are both avoided, but the Cannop stoneworks and a 'free mine' nearby add interest to the walk.

At the St. Briavels end the waymarking starts a mile along the Coleford road at Bearse Common. It continues via Roads Lane, Bream Cross, Arthur's Folly, Nagshead Nursery, Cannop Ponds, Russell's Inclosure, Speech House, Crabtree Hill, Drybrook Road 'Station', Birch Wood, Nailbridge, Harry Hill and the Beech Walk to the Wilderness. (A major diversion is imminent in the Nagshead—Cannop Ponds area.)

From the Forest Path signpost at grid ref. 659178, leave the forest through kissing gate, ignore track ahead, go half left and make for left end of high wall, then down path into Mitcheldean. If starting at Mitcheldean turn left up lane at end of raised pavement on the Drybrook road. Join ascending path up through fields, passing high wall, which keep on left. In top field, strike half left, over hump of field, to gate into the Forest, where waymarking starts.

Signposts where the path crosses roads make easy joining points. Those wishing to return to their starting point are advised to walk all or part of the $8\frac{1}{2}$ mile section from Nailbridge to Bream, utilising the Lydney to Cinderford bus service for the return journey. The bus passes Bream, Parkend, Speech House and Boey's Pike, the latter point being at the north end of Cinderford, and only $\frac{3}{4}$ mile from the waymarked path at Nailbridge school.

For further details about this route see the leaflet mentioned above under 'Waymarked Forest Paths'.

3 North-west Dean Waymarked Forest Paths

6¾ miles. Speech House - Edge End - Mile End - Cannop Ponds - Speech House

9¾ miles. Christchurch Camp Site - Edge End - Speech House - Cannop Ponds - Mile End - Christchurch

5 miles. Christchurch Camp Site - Edge End - Mile End - Christchurch

2¼ miles. Edge End - Lydbrook

Allow for travel at about 2 miles per hour. *Maps* Sheets 142, 143.

The waymarking in this area provides two links between the Highmeadow and St. Briavels–Mitcheldean routes described in the two previous rambles and utilises parts of each of these routes to form the 9¾ mile circuit. In addition, a short link one mile long between Edge End and Mile End enables the walker to follow a circular waymarked route entirely in the Forest of Dean without having to go through the semi-built-up areas of Berry Hill and Five Acres. A 2¼ mile spur route links the Forest of Dean waymarking system at Edge End picnic site with Lydbrook. There a river path and an old railway bridge over the Wye, converted into a footbridge, gives access to Bicknor Youth Hostel, and to river paths in either section to Goodrich.

Good starting points are the picnic site on the A4136 at Edge End, the Christchurch Camp Site, Speech House, Cannop Ponds and Perch Lodge at Mile End. Further details are given in the leaflet referred to under 'Waymarked Forest Paths'.

4 The south and east of the Forest of Dean. Speech House and the Roman Road at Blackpool Bridge

Distance 9¼ miles. Allow 5½ hours, including 1 hour meal break.

Maps required One inch to one mile—Nos. 143 and 155 or 156, or 1:25,000 SO/60 and 61.

Access by Bus Cinderford - Speech House - New Fancy - Parkend - Lydney. Gloucester - Cinderford - Speech House - Coleford. St. Briavels - Yorkley - Blakeney.

This walk takes the rambler into many interesting parts of the south and east of the Forest of Dean, including the Roman Road at Blackpool Bridge, and fine viewpoints at Danby Lodge and New Fancy. The route is planned to keep as far as possible to tracks marked on the one-inch maps.

From Speech House (grid reference 620121) take the Parkend and Blakeney road and at the end of the field on left, bear left into the Spruce Drive. Follow this fine avenue for about a mile. Where the gravel road turns left, keep to grass track straight on until a broad cross track is reached; keep straight on, descending to stream and ascend steeply to Staple Edge (645103). Take the path by the hedge along the left side of the foresters' houses and ignoring side turnings follow path down until a broad forest road is reached. Turn right for about 20 yards when on left descend into sunken track (not easily seen). Follow this path down to the village of Soudley. Join road by bridge, cross stream, take left fork and follow to cross roads by White Horse Inn. Keep straight on for ¼ mile until the lowest of the beautiful Soudley Ponds appears on left. Now retrace steps for 80 yards and take the left fork down narrow lane to stone bridge. Immediately over bridge fork right up to gate leading into forest. Follow right-hand path, not on one inch map, and go straight over next crossing to junction of five ways (658098) where bear half right on road, and in 80 yards turn left onto another road. You are now on one of the many Roman Roads in the Forest of Dean. After half a mile a notice on left indicates the Drummer Boy Stone, where the iron coating on part of the rock suggests early smelting. The road gradually drops to a valley, crossing a brook at Blackpool Bridge. Just beyond is an uncovered section of the Roman Road, complete with the actual stones and kerbstones (see plate 11).

Pass under old railway bridge and over the B4431 road. Take the right fork on re-entering the forest and follow steadily ascending track. Danby Lodge is just visible on the right and there are views across to the Cotswolds on the left. Cross forest road and at top of steeper ascent bear left by tall beech trees. Ignore path on left and after 150 yards bear left at old barn and keep hedge and fields on right for over ¼ mile. When fields end, take second turning on right (642077), and travel alongside electricity line for ¾ mile. Near the bottom of the path, where the electricity line turns right, keep straight on, cross line of old railway, bear left, cross road and make for Rising Sun Public House at Moseley Green (632087). From the inn, cross stile and turn left along fence for a few yards to path on right. (Do not take path leading from stile). Cross another stile into forest and keep straight on to a forest road and to road junction near "The Barracks". Follow the Speech House Road opposite for 250 yards to the foot of the old slag heaps of the New Fancy Colliery on right and left. A stiff climb up the right-hand heap, now landscaped, is rewarded by one of best panoramic views in the Forest of Dean. Returning to the aforementioned point 250 yards from the road junction, take the westwards going track, keeping fence on right for half a mile, ignoring a good left turn, to a junction of five tracks.

The old oaks at this junction are called the Three Brothers but only two are surviving. Turn right and take the left and lower of the two forest roads. After about a mile the St. Briavels to Mitcheldean waymarked forest path is joined (618111). Bear slightly right and follow the waymarking to Speech House.

---

5 Chepstow - Wintour's Leap - Tidenham Chase - Devil's Pulpit - Tintern Abbey - Wyndcliff - Chepstow

Distance 12 miles. Allow 7½ hours, including 1 hour meal break.

Maps required One inch to one mile no. 155, or 1:25,000—so/59 and a small part of so/50.

Access by bus No. 29 Coleford–Tintern or Tidenham Chase–Chepstow. No. 49 Monmouth–Tintern–St. Arvans–Chepstow.

This walk, based on the bridges over the Wye at Chepstow and Tintern, can have few equals for the sheer magnificence of its viewpoints and for the settings of the antiquities passed.

The Wye is seen from the most dramatic cliff at Wintour's Leap, and, together with a more distant view to the Bristol Channel, from the Wyndcliff. Although Tintern Abbey is much visited by tourists, its beauty may be admired in peace from parts of this walk on either side of the Wye. The route includes a fine stretch of Offa's Dyke near the Devil's Pulpit and a walk across one of Gloucestershire's last remaining heaths at Tidenham Chase. If time permits a visit to Chepstow Castle will be found most rewarding.

Starting from Chepstow Bridge climb a steep lane opposite. At the top cross A48 into road opposite. Before the first houses, cross stile on left. For the next 1½ miles you will be following part of the Offa's Dyke Long Distance Footpath, waymarked with white arrows and acorn symbols. Follow the hedge up the hill, past an old watch tower near the line of Offa's Dyke, and cross stile in far corner of field. Keep wall on left, turning left over stile at angle in wall, into narrow path for a few yards. Turn right into a drive and after 35 yards go left across a stile. Cross field to a stile at grid reference 540956, then right between railings and wall to road. Turn left, and 100 yards on follow path left through archway headed 'Moyle Old School Lane'. Walk along top of Woodcroft Quarry and on reaching the road again go left through an opening to the breathtaking viewpoint of Wintour's Leap (542962), named after Sir John Wintour, who in 1642 escaped from pursuit by Parliamentarians by jumping with his horse down the cliff and swimming the river.

A quarter mile up the road (B4228), just after Netherhope Lane on right, cross stile on right opposite house. Follow footpath marked on map through, then beside the wood. In the last field before the Dyke path rejoins the B road, at 548972, leave that route and bear right on to broad track into Boughspring. Walk past several houses, and at "No through road" sign, take enclosed path on left. Keep hedge on left in first field and on right in second field. Walk over heathland and enter woodlands called 'Parson's Allotment', probably because the land went to the Church when an old common was enclosed. Keep straight on through wood to join road near church (556988). Enter field on left opposite Rosemary Lane. Keep hedge on right, cross three stiles, and turn right into lane. Turn left before quarry entrance, follow hedge, then through gate and diagonally across field towards holly bush overgrowing stone stile. The next field should also be crossed diagonally to stile in opposite corner, and alongside hedge in next field into woods. Fifty yards diagonally left from here is the Devil's Pulpit (543995) from which the Devil is said to have preached to the monks of Tintern. Returning to where the wood was entered, follow the path just inside the wood. The mount on the right is Offa's Dyke, built in the 8th century A.D. as a boundary with Wales. After 500 yards go left down a rough path to a forest road. At junction with another forest road turn right and then, almost immediately, take path on left, down steps. Continue to descend down a steep, narrow path leading eventually to wider tracks and so across bridge to Tintern Abbey. From Tintern Abbey, take lane opposite road to abbey and bear round left along the backs of houses. Just after hotel car park, turn left at signpost to Black Cliff, up a track which gives fine views of the abbey in its magnificent setting. At the top of this track go through gate, then across field towards wooden bungalow. On reaching wire fence turn right, and shortly afterwards left, through farm yard (532994), and past the back of disused farmhouse. Follow remains of hedge on right up hill and enter wood through gate in corner. Follow track down through wood, joining main road (A466) under Black Cliff (533982). After 200 yards, just before sharp bend, re-enter wood and follow track parallel to road. Turn right onto track coming up between cottages, and soon take a steep path left up to the Wyndcliff.

After visiting this wonderful viewpoint, continue along path down to a road, onto which turn left. Join main road and follow into village of St. Arvans. Continue on main road for two miles, past the Racecourse, into Chepstow. Unfortunately the only footpath routes to avoid this road walk involve a considerable detour to the west.

6 Tintern - Botany Bay - Bigsweir - Brockweir - Tintern

Distance 9¼ miles. Allow 6 hours including a one-hour meal break.

Maps required One inch to one mile. No. 155 or 1 : 25,000 so/50.

Access by bus No. 49 Monmouth–Bigsweir–Tintern–Chepstow.

No. 29 Coleford–St. Briavels–Brockweir–Tintern–Chepstow.

No. 57 Monmouth–Botany Bay–Tintern.

This ramble utilises the crossings of the Wye at Tintern and Bigsweir and is so arranged that whilst the first part is mostly in the woodlands high up on the Monmouthshire side of the Wye, the second part is along the river banks of the Wye on the Gloucestershire side. Short cuts can be made using Brockweir Bridge. Hotels and cafes abound at Tintern and there is a Holiday Fellowship Youth Guest House and a cafe at Llandogo (accessible from the ramble by descending steeply near Cleddon Shoots).

Starting from Tintern Parva leave the main road at the Wye Valley Hotel by the lane signposted 'Catbrook'. After 100 yards cross stream and turn left by lamp-post up narrow bridle path. After climbing for 350 yards ignore uphill path on left, and continue along track ahead which bears left past cottage. Just before entering wood at top of hill, ignore branch off to right. The path climbs gently and crosses forest road and continues by edge of wood with stone wall on right. At end of wood path joins metalled road by White Cottage (Grid reference 518018). Turn sharp right, then 70 yards on turn left off road at end of wall and keep to edge of wood. In 200 yards turn right at cross paths by telephone pole, and descend steeply alongside telephone line to Botany Bay (521021).

Cross road and take ill-defined path by letter box up bracken covered hillside. In 50 yards bear right along broad grassy track through edge of wood and later open fields. On reaching road at footpath signpost 'Botany Bay 0·4 km' turn left and follow road for ½ mile to road junction. The path goes straight ahead through Bargain Wood, and is signposted 'Cleddon 1·2 km'. Ignore all side turnings and cross over stream (sign to 'Cleddon Falls' on right). Metalled road comes in from left and bears away to the right; cross this, to bridle path signposted 'Pen-y-Fan 2·4 km', keeping wall on left and follow grassy track past cottage on right. After ½ mile a clearing is reached before a conifer wood. The track crosses a major intersection at 521047 and the right hand fork leading slightly downhill should be followed. After about a mile at crossing of tracks (535050) go straight on; but if continuing onto ramble 7 bear left

Plate 49. The Scowles: Roman workings for iron ore in the Crease Limestone near Bream

Plate 5o. The westward view from the Buckstone near Staunton, over the Wye Valley towards the Black Mountains of Breconshire in South Wales

Plate 52. And doggie came too!

Plate 53. Common lizard

Plate 54. Toad

Plate 55. Slow worm

Plate 56. Quarry in the Lower Dolomite Limestone at Plump Hill

Plate 57. The Near Hearkening Rock in the Highmeadow Woods, a sandstone bluff famous for its echoes.

Plate 58. Nestling cuckoo, well camouflaged in a Tree Pipit's nest

and follow that way to Pen-y-Fan Common. For Bigsweir however after 70 yards turn sharp right onto narrow woodland path which descends, crossing a track and continuing down to the main road. At footpath signpost "Pen-y-Fan 1·6 km" turn left for Bigsweir Bridge.

After crossing Bigsweir Bridge, go immediately right over stile. (The path from here to Brockweir is a section of the Offa's Dyke Long Distance Footpath and is waymarked with the acorn symbol). Follow river bank downstream passing in front of Bigsweir House. Keep close to river through wood. In the fields on the bend of the river opposite Llandogo be particularly careful to keep to the river path and to avoid trampling any mowing grass. Follow the river path all the way to Brockweir. Turn left by the bridge, and opposite Post Office turn right, past New Inn. Just before road crosses stream, turn right down path between houses. Follow this path into field over stile. Cross field bearing slightly left, making for hedge on left. Cross hedge approximately where electricity wires cross field. Join track and turn right along it into wood. Half a mile beyond entrance to wood, the track 'hairpins' left, but go straight on down steep path onto old tramway track. Bear right onto this and go on and over bridge to Tintern. Turn left for the Abbey, and right for the starting point.

---

7 Bigsweir - Whitebrook - Redbrook - Newland - St Briavels - Bigsweir

Distance 10¾ miles (*3½ miles on the west side of the Wye, and 7¼ miles on the east side*). Allow about 6½ hours including one hour for meal break.

Maps required One inch to one mile, nos. 142 and 155, or 1: 25,000: so/50 and so/51.

Access by bus No. 49 Monmouth–Redbrook–Chepstow.
No. 33 Coleford–Newland–Redbrook–Monmouth.
No. 29 Coleford–Mork–St. Briavels–Chepstow.

This ramble, as with most of the other rambles in this series, contains a pleasant mixture of river, woodland and upland scenery together with great historical interest, provided in this instance by St. Briavels Castle, Newland Church (the 'Cathedral of the Forest'), and the remains of the Great Oak at Newland.

Starting from the old railway station at Bigsweir Bridge, take the Whitebrook road northwards. At the end of the wood on left, take line of path signposted 'Pen-y-Fan 0·8 km', striking diagonally across field and several fences to enter wood over stile which lies straight up the hill from the farm. Follow path in wood, turning right where paths cross. Follow path to Pen-y-Fan common at GR. 534061. A short detour may be made right to the maypole, otherwise cross the common keeping large tree and houses on right, and descend by rough track into Whitebrook. Turn left at minor road and go 100 yards up the road, right over stream and fork right onto track up through a wood. After 300 yards, near end of field on right, and just past slight bend, watch for small path descending steeply on right to join a wider track leading in 400 yards to bridge under old railway onto river bank. Turn left and follow river path for $1\frac{3}{4}$ miles to Redbrook railway bridge. Go under bridge, turn sharp left, past Boat Inn and over river by footbridge attached to disused railway bridge and so into Redbrook (inns and cafes).

Go north on the Monmouth Road and bear right on unmade road opposite Wye Valley Garage and Cafe to join B4231. Go up the hill for $\frac{1}{2}$ mile and just after passing millpond on right, turn right and cross footbridge. Pass up to stile beyond and into field. Bear slightly left and enter wood at its corner jutting into field (no stile at time of writing). Inside wood follow left edge at first, then path rises to a stile into field. Pass to right of wood on left and go through gate. Keep fence on right and go over high stile by a gate on right. Hedge is now on left for the three and a half fields. Cross diagonal-running fence and keep hedge now on right. Away in the next field to the right is the remains of the Great Oak of Newland, believed to be a thousand years old. With a girth of 44 feet, it was, when in its prime, the largest in Britain, but it was struck by lightning in 1955. Pass through gate and in the last field bear right to join road to the left of farm buildings. Turn right into Newland (inn).

The large church at Newland was once the parish church for the whole Forest of Dean, and has many interesting features, particularly the miners' brass to be found under a carpet in the Greyndour Chapel, and the tomb of a Forester (see page 115). Leave churchyard by the south-west corner, passing almhouses on left, and go down steep road. At bottom of hill turn right and in 50 yards bear left over cattle grid. Follow rough road along valley for about a mile. After crossing stream by a bridge, follow track past front of Lodges Farm (549078), and through fieldgate into large field. The line of the path bears diagonally left to enter wood about 100 yards left of where electricity transmission line crosses. Path is indistinct at first, but clear where it runs diagonally left to stile at top of wood. Old line of path passes to right of buildings and follows access road to lane, but may be diverted to follow field boundaries and join access road midway between buildings and lane. Bear left onto lane and pass Wyegate Green, descending narrowing lane to Mork (ignore tracks to right). Cross road, and stream and follow lane up Mork Hill into St. Briavels.

St. Briavels Castle is now a Youth Hostel but it is not otherwise open to the public. Take the minor road westwards from the castle, signposted to Lower Mesne. This descends to a cross roads at 555044, where continue with pillar box on left. Ignore branching-off right, and follow road which bears right, with a cottage on right. Continue on road for 300 yards leaving it where it turns sharply right and carry on along path. At gate, go left and take right-hand path following lower boundary of wood. Pass along side of field with wood on right. A slight mound in that wood is part of Offa's Dyke. Cross stile into next field and follow path along line of ancient sweet chestnuts. Five trees from the end of the line turn right through gate and cross field diagonally left to join drive near cattle grid. If joining Ramble 8, turn left, but for Bigsweir Bridge turn right and follow drive to main road.

---

8 Monmouth - The Kymin - Redbrook - Penallt - Monmouth

Distance 7 miles. Allow about 3½ hours, without break.

Maps One inch to one mile, no. 142 or 1 : 25,000 so/51 and small part of so/50.

Access by bus No. 49 Monmouth–Redbrook–Chepstow.
No. 33 Coleford–Redbrook–Monmouth.

This, the shortest of our series of rambles, starts with a climb from Monmouth to the Kymin, with its Naval Temple and fine view. The Wye is crossed by the useful footbridge at Redbrook and a return to Monmouth can be made either by going up past the quaint little church at Penallt and another good viewpoint at Troypark Wood, or by a more leisurely route along the river bank.

From the Wye Bridge at Monmouth take the Gloucester (A4136) road, and shortly after that road turns left at the May Hill Hotel, bear right on upper side of road, ignoring first path on right. Pass through a wood, then alongside a field and up a minor road. Where road turns right take path on left of garage and ascend for 300 yards by path (not marked on one-inch maps) to point at grid reference 526130; turn right over stile. Ascend field bearing left to house at top corner. Go over stiles and follow path over a stile up through new plantation to emerge into a sunken lane and so onto the top of the hill (National Trust). Note the Kymin Round House and the curious Naval Temple further on, built in 1800 to commemorate Nelson's admirals. The fine view from the Kymin includes the Black Mountains and the Brecon Beacons of South Wales.

Follow path due south from the Naval Temple. Pass through the kissing gate on the left and follow footpath alongside fence and then to the right of three fields. Enter lane by a barn at 530116. Follow this lane downhill one mile to a road (B4231), turn right and follow down to Redbrook. Turn left at bottom of hill for centre of village (cafes and inn).

From Lower Redbrook, opposite Post Office, take path past football field and cross Wye by footbridge attached to the disused railway bridge. Turn right, pass by the Boat Inn and follow riverside path for ¼ mile. If following river path to Monmouth carry straight on; but for the Penallt Church route, turn left at end of wall on left, pass left of a house and up narrow road, turning right after 200 yards. Keep straight on for ½ mile along lane, which becomes a path at last house. If path overgrown bear right and then left to gate in top corner of paddock. Follow path to minor road and up to Penallt Church. Go round the back of the church, over stone stile and follow enclosed path emerging onto wider track. Pass through gate and along right side of two fields straight into Troypark Wood. 100 yards into wood, path turns down left near yew trees, and descends to wide track, onto which turn left. After 80 yards cross stile on right into field below and strike diagonally left to gate in opposite corner. Bear right to keep hedge on right in next field, then bear right again into next field and pass to the left of Troy Farm and House, joining old A40 at end of main drive. Turn right and bear right at houses. Go underneath dual carriageway, climb steps to cross River Monnow by side of road and descend to follow path across park to Monmouth town centre.

9 Monmouth - Kymin - Buckstone - Biblins - Dixton-Monmouth

Distance 9 miles (9½ with Seven Sisters Rocks and King Arthur's Cave). Allow 5½ hours with one hour meal break (6¼ hours with diversion).

Maps required One inch to one mile, no. 142, or 1 : 25,000 so/51.

Access by bus No. 40 Lydney–Coleford–Staunton–Monmouth–Hereford.

Although overlapping with two other rambles, this ramble is worthy of inclusion by virtue of its immense variety of terrain and its magnificent scenery throughout. It includes a long though delightful stretch of river-side walking, a most interesting section of the Highmeadow Waymarked Forest Path, and climbs up to the viewpoints of the Kymin and the Buckstone. The climbing is done in the early part of the ramble and the riverside walking in the latter part—a pleasant arrangement for a hot summer's day.

From the Wye Bridge at Monmouth follow the instructions for ramble number 8 as far as the Kymin.

Leaving the Kymin property by the north-east corner over stile, follow right-hand fence, bearing slightly left on nearing farm buildings. Go over stile by a detached house and turn left along lane. In 100 yards turn right down to main road, (A4136) where, bearing right 300 yards on, turn right up steep path just inside wood. Go over cross tracks, bearing slightly right to path on left up to gate in gap between two woods. Pass by the Buckstone Adventure Centre on right and then in front of a red house (Buckstone Lodge). Turn left beyond house and up hill to stile in wall. Cross stile to the Buckstone.

This huge stone used to rock before it was dislodged in 1885. From this point of 915 feet altitude there is a fine panoramic view over the Forest of Dean, Highmeadow Woods and away to the Black Mountains.

Return to the stile and turn left on to the waymarked path down into Staunton. See ramble 1 for further details about the Highmeadow Waymarked Forest Path, which is followed past the Suckstone and Near Hearkening Rock, then descends steeply through the Ecological Reserve in Lady Park Wood (see page 66) to the Biblins suspension footbridge (grid reference 549144). Cross bridge, turn left and commence four miles of grand river path which goes all the way to Monmouth. Diversions can be made from the riverside, firstly up the steep waymarked route to the Seven Sisters Rocks and King Arthur's Cave, and secondly, nearer Monmouth to the small and much flooded church at Dixton.

---

10 Symonds Yat Rock - English Bicknor - Lydbrook - Kerne Bridge - Goodrich Castle - Huntsham Bridge - Symonds Yat Rock

Distance 10 miles. Allow 6½ hours, including 1 hour for meal break and half hour Goodrich Castle.

Maps required One inch to one mile, no. 142 or 1 : 25,000 so/51.

Access by bus No. 35 Ross–Kerne Bridge–Lydbrook–Christchurch–Coleford. No. 36 Coleford–Symonds Yat Rock. No. 60 Newport –Monmouth–Goodrich Cross–Ross–Gloucester.

This delightful ramble takes advantage of the tremendous bends of the Wye in the Symonds Yat and Lydbrook districts and provides two sections of riverside walking as well as spectacular viewpoints like Symonds Yat Rock and Coldwell Rocks. A visit should be made to Goodrich Castle (in the charge of the Department of the Environment, and open daily), and to the old churches of English Bicknor and Goodrich.

After admiring the view from Symonds Yat Rock, return to the road and take level path starting parallel with the same side of the road. After half mile cross small streams at grid reference 569155. Path bends left over stile; and at fork take left-hand path leading past Ship and Needle Rocks. Having come a mile through wood, leave it by stile at signboard high on tree: 'To English Bicknor'.

Cross field diagonally and follow right-hand hedge and wall, bearing right, over stile, down through plantation to minor road. Turn right, then left up road, and, just past cottages, path on left leads up short avenue to church (note Norman arch by pulpit). Through lych gate, turn left down road for $\frac{1}{4}$ mile. Before cottages on left bear left into field and follow right hedge, through two fields. On entering open field keep straight on, making for stile by gate in line with distant red roof. Go down next field with hedge on left. At gap at bottom turn left and after 100 yards turn right onto farm track. Go over stile by gate in cutting, then pass through section of Offa's Dyke and follow farm road down to B4228. Pass factory entrance on left, then by bus stop turn left on signposted path to river and cross Wye by footway over old railway bridge. On leaving bridge turn right along river path, passing Welsh Bicknor Youth Hostel. Continue along riverpath for $3\frac{1}{2}$ miles to Kerne Bridge where turn left up road, then up path and steps to bridge over road. Turn right into Goodrich. Follow signposted path for $\frac{1}{2}$ mile to the Castle.

Returning to village take road opposite castle path, then follow path to right over school playing field and sloping fields to church. Go right round the church to the north west corner of the churchyard by house and tall trees and up to a road. A few yards to right turn sharp left behind cottages onto path alongside orchard, leading down through rough fields to Goodrich Cross (Cross Keys Inn). Turn left on track, pass right of farm, then down past fine old oak to spring at bottom of field (wood on right). Cross fence, then follow right-hand fence to stile. Go down next field to B4229. Take road opposite and go over Huntsham Bridge. Turn left along Wye for a mile. Pass big boulders by river and two cottages. Keep on path through wood. Towards end of rough clearing below on left, path slopes gently up away from river. After ruined cottage, path goes steeply up to forest road, which cross and continue up steps opposite. When path meets another one turn right and follow zig-zag up to road. 200 yards up steep road brings one back to Symonds Yat Rock.

11 Longhope - May Hill - Longhope

Distance 5 miles. Allow 2½ hours.

Maps required One inch to one mile 143 or 1 : 25,000 sheets so61, 62, 71, 72.

Access by bus No. 24 Gloucester–Longhope–Cinderford (also Cottrells Coaches).

No. 38 Gloucester–Huntley–Nag's Head–Ross.

Note : Only the general situation of this walk is indicated at (11) on the front endpaper map.)

This ramble is to the summit of May Hill, Gloucestershire's most easily identified hill. The clump of trees on top were planted to celebrate Queen Victoria's golden jubilee in 1887. It forms a convenient half day walk starting and finishing in the pleasant valley at Longhope.

Starting at Longhope church, at so/684198, go along the road northwards to where the A40 turns into it, Opposite the Nags Head Inn turn right onto path across field to crossing over old railway in a dip left through an orchard onto a minor road. Turn right, then right again up a lane between farm buildings. When the lane bends left, go up beside some cottages over a stile and up the hill, bearing right across the field, then up steps over a steep bank. Bear right through a small wood at top of next field, then up the fields beyond, keeping the hedge on the right. Go past May Hill Farm and up a green lane through a gate to a minor road. To the left of the house opposite the gate, clear path goes to the top of May Hill. At the Ordnance Survey's trig. point, turn south-east, going down a track with conifers on the left. Take right fork at cross tracks, then fork right again down a narrow gulley, which becomes a green lane, turns left, then becomes a rough road. At minor road, turn left, follow the sign to the right for Dursley Cross (inn), then bear left to the main road (A40). Turn right, and in about 300 yards take a lane to the left. Where the lane bends right keep ahead on the path inside the wood with hedge on left for about a mile. When a stile is visible below and to the left of the path (695190), take a path on the right going diagonally down into the wood. Keep right and go up a slope to a stile into a field. Ignore gate, and with the hedge at first on the right, continue south-west down hill over three fields, bearing left at bottom to cross a stile into a rough lane leading to road (A4136) near the Plough Inn.

Follow road over old railway bridge (due for demolition and road widening at time of writing), then left down minor road and by bridge

Longhope Brook. Go through gate into field on right, make for gap in hedge ahead, straight on to stile followed by stone over stream at next hedge, then in direction of wooded hill, make for gap with gate beyond. Bear right and cross new section of A.4136 by stiles into orchard. Keep hedge, then garden, on right to reach road 686187. Go up tarred lane opposite. This terminates in short grass lane, leading into orchard which follow on upper side to stiles at crossing of narrow road. In next field make for gap, then, with hedge on right, proceed to stile/gate onto lane which turns right. After 60 yards leave narrow lane over footbridge, and make for white kissing gate. Turn right onto road and so down to Longhope church.

12   Offa's Dyke Long Distance Footpath

The Offa's Dyke Path is an official Long Distance Footpath created under the National Parks and Access to the Countryside Act 1949. It runs for 168 miles from the Severn Estuary at Sedbury Cliff to Prestatyn on the North Wales coast. For most of its length it follows Offa's Dyke, an earthwork constructed by King Offa of Mercia in the eighth century A.D. as a boundary mark between his kingdom and Wales.

The extent of preservation of the mound, and its accompanying ditch, varies greatly in the Lower Wye Valley. The best preserved and most continuous sections are in the woods opposite, and to the south-east of, Tintern Abbey. Another good stretch is from The Fence, north-east of Bigsweir and on past Coxbury Farm. Good isolated sections can be seen at Sedbury and at Madgett Hill, east of Brockweir. Across St. Briavels Common and the Hudnalls area only fragmentary remains exist and there are in fact two official routes for the long distance path, the alternative being the attractive path alongside the River Wye between Bigsweir and Brocksweir. North of Redbrook and for the next 53 miles to Rushock Hill, near Kington, the official path follows a planned route and not any line of the ancient dyke, which was never built across the forests of Herefordshire. Isolated fragments of the Dyke, which are not parts of the official path, can be seen on rambles 1 and 10 at Symonds Yat and at Stowfield, to the west of Lydbrook.

Several of the rambles described above can be varied by using the Offa's Dyke Path. No stile-by-stile account is given here because the route is waymarked with white arrows, acorn symbols and signposts. Strip maps showing the exact route on scale of 1 : 25,000 (2½ inches to 1 mile) can be obtained from the Offa's Dyke Association, Knighton, Radnorshire (Send stamped addressed envelope for details of these and other publications by the Association).

Books on the Forest of Dean

Compiled by Dr. C.E.Hart

The literature is more extensive than is generally realized, but, unfortunately, nearly all of the earlier works are out of print. Copies are, however, obtainable through public libraries, or may occasionally be picked up second hand.

Baty, F. W. *Forest of Dean*. Robert Hale, London. 1952. 90p.

Bellows, J. *A Week's Holiday in the Forest of Dean* One of the most successful little guides ever written. Very useful to the tourist. Latest edition 1965, published by John Bellows Ltd., Gloucester. 12½p. Illustrated. Map.

Bevan, Tom. *The Thane of Dean*. Fiction. Partridge, London. (No date).

Boevey, Catharina. *The Perverse Widow*. An account of life at Flaxley in the eighteenth century. 1898. Illustrated.

Bradley and Palmer. *The Wye*. A. and C. Black. 1926.

Bright, Thomas. *The Rise of Nonconformity in the Forest of Dean*. The Forest Newspapers Ltd., Coleford, Glos. 1954. 25p.

——*Bell's: The Story of a Gloucestershire School*. The Forest Newspapers Ltd., Coleford, Gloucester. 25p.

Cooke, A. O. *The Forest of Dean*. Good descriptions of the scenery. 1913. Illustrated.

Cooper, Gordon. *A Fortnight in the Wye Valley*. Percival Marshall, 1951.

Cox, J. C. *The Royal Forests of England*. General account of the forests. Brief chapter (XXII) on Dean. 1905. Illustrated.

Crawley-Boevey, S. M. *Dene Forest Sketches*. Series I and II. Historical and biographical, based on documents at Flaxley Abbey. Ser. II, 1890. Illustrated. (Ser. I).

Crawley-Boevey, A. W. *The Cartulary and Historical Notes of the Cistercian Abbey of Flaxley*. Many documents of which are printed. 1887. Illustrated.

Ducarel, P. J. *De Wyrhale*. Historical fiction in verse. 1836. Illustrated.

Edlin, H. L. Editor. *Dean Forest and Wye Valley*. Forest Park Guide. HMSO. First edition. 1947.

Forestry Commission. *Report of the National Forest Park Committee (Forest of Dean)* 1938. HMSO. 1938. (Cmnd 686).

—— *Report of the Forest of Dean Committee* 1958. Cmd. 686. HMSO. 1959. 40p.

Fox, Sir Cyril. *Archaeologia Cambrensis*, Vol. 86. An important scientific study of the part of Offa's Dyke skirting the Forest.

Gloucester, City of. *Official Guide to Gloucester, 1967*. British Publishing Co. Gloucester.

Grindrod, C. *Tales in the Speech-House*. Fiction. 1886.

Hart, Cyril E. MA, PH D. *The Extent and Boundaries of The Forest of Dean and Hundred of St. Briavels*. Bellows, Gloucester. 1947. 25p.

The Verderers and Speech-Court of the Forest of Dean. Bellows, Gloucester. 1950. 50p.

The Commoners of Dean Forest. British Publishing Co. Gloucester. 1951. 75p.

Laws of Dean. British Publishing Co. Gloucester. 1952. 37½p.

The Free Miners of the Royal Forest of Dean and Hundreds of St. Briavels. British Publishing Co. Gloucester. 1953. £1.05.

Archaeology in Dean. Bellows, Gloucester, 1967. £1.05. Illustrated.

Royal Forest. Oxford University Press. 1966. Illustrated. The definitive history for the Dean. £3.75.

The Industrial History of Dean. David and Charles. Newton Abbot, 1971. £6.50. Illustrated.

The Verderers and Forest Laws of Dean. David and Charles, Newton Abbot, 1971. £3.15. Illustrated.

Hill, H. C. *Report on the Forest of Dean* with suggestions for its management HMSO. 1897.

Holmes, A. Dorothy. *Severn, Dean and Wye Valley.* Wildings, Shrewsbury. 1946. Illustrated. 75p.

Moore, John. *The White Sparrow.* Fiction. Collins, London. 1954. 52½p.

Moore, J. C. *The Welsh Marches.* Chapman & Hall, London. 1933.

Mountjoy, Timothy. *The Life, Labours and Deliverances of a Forest of Dean Collier.* Of no literary merit, but valuable as a collier's record of the life of the Forest in the nineteenth century. 1887.

Mansfield, R. J. *Forest Story: Dean Forest through the Ages.* 1964. Published at The Vicarage, Newnham, Gloucester.

Nicholls, Rev. H. G. *An Historical and Descriptive Account of the Forest of Dean.* Not up to modern standards of historiography, but still valuable. 1858. Illustrated. Maps. Re-issued in 1966 by David and Charles, Newton Abbot at £2.50. Edited by C. E. Hart. New title: *Nicholl's Forest of Dean.*

The Personalities of the Forest of Dean. Useful biographical sketches of Forest officials and others. 1863.

Iron Making in the Olden Times. Valuable for the history of the industry, particularly by the inclusion of the 'Book of Dennis', which gives the laws of the Free Miners. 1886. Illustrated. Re-issued in 1966 as part of *Nicholl's Forest of Dean*—See above.

Ormerod, G. *Strigulensia.* Archaeological notes on the Chepstow area.
Osborn, Fred. M. *The Story of the Mushets.* Nelson, London. 1951. £1.05.
Paar, H. W. *The Severn and Wye Railway.* David and Charles, Newton Abbot. 1972. Illustrated.

The Great Western Railway, David and Charles, Newton Abbot, 1964.

Reid, Capt. Mayne. *No Quarter.* A story of the Civil War as it affected the Forest. Historical fiction with good local colour. 1887.

Rodgers, John. *English Woodland.* General account of woodland; brief chapter (X) on Dean. 1941.

Seebohm, F. *The English Village Community.* Chapter V deals with Tidenham, which is a *locus classicus* of English social history. Used by Maitland and others. 1883. Map.

Sibley, T. Franklin. *Iron Ores—the Haematites of the Forest of Dean and South Wales.* (Memoirs of the Geological Survey). HMSO, 2nd Edition 1927.

Sopwith, T. *The Award of the Dean Forest Mining Commissioners, etc.* 1841. Map of mines.

Thoresby Jones. *Welsh Border Country.* Batsford. 1958.

Trotter, A. W. *The Dean Road*. An account of the Roman road across the Forest. 1936. Illustrated. Map.

Trotter, F. M. *Geology of the Forest of Dean Coal and Iron-ore Field*. (Memoirs of the Geological Survey). HMSO 1942.

Waters, Brian. *The Forest of Dean*. Dent, London. 1951. 75p.

Wheeler, R. E. M. & T. V. *Report on the Excavation of the Prehistoric, Roman, and Post-Roman Site in Lydney Park*. Important to students of the period. 1932. Illustrated and plans.

Wood, J. G. *The Laws of Dean Forest*. A valuable compendium of legal and historical documents. 1878.

Woods, Mabel K. *Newnham-on-Severn. A Retrospect*. Bellows, Gloucester. 1912. Second edition 1962, published at: The Vicarage, Newnham, Gloucester.

Wyedean Guide. 1973. Wyedean Tourist Board, Ross-on-Wye.

General

Transactions of the Bristol and Gloucestershire Archaeological Society. Many articles of value. Current. Illustrated.

Report of the National Forest Park Committee (Forest of Dean). HMSO 1938.

Victoria County History of Gloucestershire. Vol. II. Good articles on the industries of the Forest. 1907.

Books on Monmouth, Chepstow and the Wye

Clark, Arthur. *Raglan Castle and the Civil War in Monmouthshire*. 1953. *Chepstow, its Castle and Lordship, The Castle of St. Briavels*. 1949.

Davies, E. T. *History of the Parish of Mathern*. 1950.

Dicker, J. J. *Life in Hewelsfield and Brocksweir during the 16th Century*. 1950.

Evans, C. J. O. *Monmouthshire, its History and Topography*. Lewis, Cardiff. 1953.

Evans, H. A. *Monmouthshire*. Cambridge University Press. 1915.

Farr, Grahame E. *Chepstow Ships*. 1954.

Gibbings, Robert. *Coming Down the Wye*. Illustrated.

Gilbert, H. A. *The Tale of a Wye Fisherman*.

Hando, Fred. *This Pleasant Land of Gwent*. Illustrated. R. H. Johns, Newport. 1944. 42½p

Hutton, E. *A Book of the Wye*.

Mee, Arthur (Edit.). *Monmouthshire*. Hodder & Stoughton, London. 1951.

Morris, A. *Geography and History of Monmouthshire*. Dawson, Newport. 1901. *Official Guide to Monmouthshire*.

Waters, Ivor. *Chepstow Miscellany*. 1958. *About Chepstow*. 1952. *Inns and Taverns of the Chepstow District*. 1949. *Chepstow Parish Records*. 1953. *A Chepstow and Tintern Anthology*. 1948. *Chepstow Town Gate*.

General information

Accommodation

The Dean and Wye Valley districts are well supplied with holiday accommodation of every kind from hotels to camp sites, conveniently situated in or near small towns and villages close to railway and bus routes. An *Accommodation List* is obtainable on request from: The Secretary, Wyedean Tourist Board, Gloucester Road, Ross-on-Wye, Herefordshire. (Phone Ross 2768). This association also publishes a useful illustrated *Wyedean Guide* wherein advertisements of many hotels and boarding houses may be found. This guide may be obtained direct from the Board or through booksellers; it covers the Wye from source to mouth.

Hotels

A brief list of the main hotels at the centres most convenient for the park appears below, but it will be appreciated that space can only be found for a small proportion. *Beachley*, Beachley Ferry. *Chepstow*, Beaufort, George, Saint Pierre. *Cinderford*, White Hart. *Coleford*, Speech House. *Drybrook*, Euroclydon. *Goodrich*, Castle View, Ye Hostelrie. *Littledean*, Littledean. *Llandogo*, Old Farmhouse. *Longhope*, Manor House. *Lydney*, Feathers. *Mitcheldean*, Ferneyfield. *Monmouth*, Angel, Beaufort Arms, King's Head, Royal George, White Swan. *Newnham*, Victoria. *Ross-on-Wye*, Chase, Chasedale, King's Head, Merton, Pengethley, Rosswyn, Royal, Swan, Valley, Wye. *St. Arvans*, Piercefield. *Staunton*, Elms. *Symonds Yat*, Paddocks, Wye Rapids, Royal. *Tintern*, Beaufort, Rose and Crown, Royal George. *Whitchurch, nr. Symonds Yat*, Doward. *Ledbury*, Feathers, Old Talbot.

Youth Hostels

The following hostels are conveniently situated for visitors to the Forest Park. Further details appear in the Association's Handbook, price 5p (7½p post free), obtainable from the Secretary, YHA, 8 St. Stephen's Hill, St. Albans.

Mitcheldean: Lion House.

St. Briavels: The Castle.

Chepstow: Mounton Road.

Welsh Bicknor: The Rectory.

Christchurch, near Coleford

Open week before Easter to third week of November.
Here in the Royal and ancient Forest of Dean are two large Class A
sites, one at Christchurch which has an extension into the adjoining
woodlands with individual pitches, and one at Bracelands ¼ mile away
with views over the River Wye. At Worcester Lodge a Class B site
has been provided in a parkland situation.

All bookings should be made on arrival at Christchurch.

The Christchurch site lies on the west side of the Coleford–
Symonds Yat road (B4432), the turn-off about one mile north of
Coleford being well signposted with international camping signs.

Address: Forest Park Camp, Christchurch, Coleford, Gloucestershire.
(Grid ref: so 569129).

Advance bookings, at Bank Holiday periods only, are accepted in
writing at least 14 days in advance for an additional fee of £1.00 to
Forestry Commission Camp Site, Christchurch, Coleford, Gloucestershire.

Charges–1972

Class A Sites and Woodland Sites
Adults 20p per night
Children (5–15 years) 10p per night

Class B Sites
Adults 10p per night
Children (5–15 years) 5p per night

These prices are subject to periodical change

The facilities include a water supply, shelter hut, ablution huts and
sanitary arrangements with wash basins and hot and cold showers.
The sites are on a good road, are well-drained and are close to wide
views over the Wye Valley. They are recommended by the Camping
Club of Great Britain and Ireland. Outside the camp sites, but near at
hand, the visitor will find a cafe, a garage, a church, and two inns.

These camp sites lie on the west of the Coleford–Symonds Yat road
at Christchurch, close to the cross-roads marked on maps as Berry
Hill. Travellers on the main Monmouth–Gloucester road should
turn north at New Inn cross-roads to reach them. The No. 40 bus
service from Lydney Junction Station to Monmouth runs past the
camp site. The no. 31 service from Gloucester through Cinderford to
Coleford also passes the camp sites, and so does the no. 35 from Ross-
on-Wye to Coleford.

Camping grounds and adventure centres for Youth Organisations, including Scouts, Guides, and school parties, are situated at: Soudley, Astonbridgehill near Lydbrook, the Hollies and Biblins south of Symonds Yat, Braceland and the Buckstone in the High-meadow Woods, and at Worcester Lodge. Enquiries regarding their use should be made to the Forestry Commission, Crown Offices, Coleford, Glos.

Car park at Symonds Yat Rock

At the famous viewpoint on the summit of the limestone cliffs of Symonds Yat, a public car park has been provided by the Forestry Commission. This is situated 2 miles north of the camp site on the road to Goodrich.

Local industries

The Forest of Dean and its environs holds, amid its sylvan beauty, a surprising range of industries. The decline of the coalfield brought a challenge to the district, which was ably met by enterprising local industrialists and their Development Association. Active, progressive industries today include:

Coal mining - *By Free Miners on the Forests' fringes.*
Stone quarrying - *At Longhope, Tidenham, Symonds Yat, and Coleford*
Engineering - *Chepstow, Cinderford, Coleford, Lydbrook, Lydney.*
Iron foundries - *Cinderford.*
Pin-making - *Whitecroft and Lydney.*
Boiler works - *Sling, near Coleford.*
Wood turning - *Longhope.*
Sawmills - *Walford, Longhope, Ruardean, Monmouth, Parkend, Cinderford, Drybrook, Lydney, Huntley and Ross.*
Plywood mills - *Lydney.*
Brush making - *Chepstow, Cinderford.*
Fruit juices - *Coleford.*
Salmon and Eel fisheries - *Along the Severn.*
Hand weaving - *Ross.*
Rubber manufacturers - *Lydney.*
Chipboard and moulded containers - *Coleford.*
Carboard packaging - *Lydbrook.*
Paper-pulp - *Sudbrook near Chepstow (Hardwood).*
Precious metals - *Cinderford.*
Industrial lubricants - *Bream.*
Photographic materials - *Mitcheldean.*
Brickworks - *Cinderford.*
Diesel engines - *Cinderford.*

Bathing

There are no organised facilities in the Forest Park. Bathing is possible, however, in the River Wye below Symonds Yat and some of the Forest of Dean pools, such as the *Lower Pool* at Soudley, but these waters are only suitable for strong swimmers. There are freshwater open-air baths at Lydney (on the Aylburton road).

Boating

Boats may be hired on the River Wye at Ross and Symonds Yat.

Early closing days

At Chepstow and Ross-on-Wye, the early closing day is *Wednesday*. At Coleford, Cinderford, Monmouth, Tintern, and Lydney, early closing is on *Thursday*.

Maps

In the Ordnance Survey one-inch series, the whole of the Park is shown on the *Wye Valley and Lower Severn Tourist Map*. The north-west appears on sheet 142, the north-east on sheet 143, and the south on sheet 155.

In Messrs. Bartholomew's half-inch series, the whole area is included on Sheet 13, *Wye Valley*.

Approach roads (see map, page xii)

Recent road improvements have brought the Forest Park within easy travelling distance from several centres. It can now be reached in 3 hours from London, 1½ from Birmingham, 1 from Cardiff, and little more than half an hour from Newport, Gloucester, Hereford or Bristol.

A Forester's Tomb in Newland Church

Briefly, there are four points of main road entry to the Park, thus:

(1) Severn Bridge and Chepstow.

(2) Gloucester.

(3) Ross-on-Wye.

(4) Monmouth.

Details follow, but first a note of caution. Though the Park is easily reached, or passed, by fast main roads, all the roads within it are narrow, steep, and winding. They call for care throughout, and the superb scenery is best enjoyed from a lay-by, rather than from the driving seat!

---

1 *By Severn Bridge from London, Bristol and southern England*

The best route from London and all parts of England south of Gloucester is over the Severn Bridge. This crosses from Aust, north of Bristol, to Beachley, close to Chepstow. Its central span, 1 mile long, makes it the seventh longest bridge in the world. There are two side spans each 1,000 feet long, one of which crosses the River Wye, close to its junction with the Severn. The towers that carry the suspension cables are 400 feet high, the cables are 20 inches thick, and the Bridge holds 13,000 tons of steel. The highway across it is a motorway, part of the M4 linking London with South Wales.

A footway is provided for pedestrians and there is also a cycle track. Toll charges are: cars, 12p, solo motor cycles 5p (1973)

From London the distance to the western, Monmouthshire end of the Bridge is 122 miles by the motorway, M4. An alternative way involving minimum use of motorways, is to take the Bath Road, A4, via Reading and Marlborough to Chippenham. Then A40 (signposted Bristol) for 10 miles to Cold Ashton. Then right turn on to A46, signposted 'M4', for 5 miles. Next a left-hand turn on to the motorway and a speedy run down to the Bridge.

From Bristol, take A38, signposted Gloucester, north until a left-hand turn to the Bridge is reached. Distance to western end: 15 miles.

On leaving the Bridge, take the first exit left, signposted Chepstow. At the first major cross roads, one mile from the exit roundabout, you may go straight on for the Wye Valley road, A466, to Tintern, Monmouth, and Ross-on-Wye. Or turn right on to the A48 for Chepstow Town, Lydney, and Gloucester.

For the Camp Site, take the A466 almost to Monmouth town, then right along A4136 (signposted Gloucester) to Lower Berry Hill. Here, at the New Inn cross-roads, turn left for the camp site.

2 Through Gloucester from London or the Midlands

Gloucester, an old cathedral city, stands at the old bridgehead over the Severn. It is 105 miles from London.

2(a) THE ROSS ROAD

The main road west, A40, runs via Huntley to Ross-on-Wye, skirting the northern edge of the Forest of Dean.

2(b) THE MONMOUTH ROAD

At Huntley, another main road, A4136, diverges left for Monmouth. This runs right through the heart of the Dean Forest, and at Lower Berry Hill (1 mile north of Coleford) passes within 1 mile of the Christchurch Camp Site (right turn at New Inn cross-roads). Beyond the New Inn, this road descends to the Wye Valley. Just before you reach Monmouth town, a left-hand turn leads to Tintern and Chepstow, or a right-hand turn to Ross-on-Wye.

2(c) THE CHEPSTOW ROAD

Three miles out of Gloucester a left-hand turn on to A48 leads to Newnham, Blakeney, Lydney, and Chepstow. Most of the roads that diverge north-west (right) from this lead deep into the Forest Park. At Chepstow, there is a link with the A466 road up the Wye Valley. Turn right (traffic lights) immediately after passing through the stone archway in Chepstow's main street.

---

3 By the M50 motorway from the Midlands to Ross-On-Wye

This very quick modern route brings Birmingham within 56 miles of Ross-on-Wye. At the end of the motorway, you may continue along the excellent trunk road, A40, to Monmouth, and there turn left for Chepstow and the lower Wye Valley via A466.

From the motorway to the Camp Site, the most attractive road is through Ross town and then via B4228 through Walford and English Bicknor to Berry Hill. There, a right-hand turn (signposted) leads to the Camp Site. Ross is also the best point of entry from Hereford (by A49) and points north.

---

4 From Newport and South Wales

There is a choice of two routes: 4(a), (b) and (c) below.

4(a) VIA MONMOUTH

Take the A40 road through Usk to Monmouth town. From that point, you may continue on the A40 north-east towards Ross.

Or take the A4136 due east from Monmouth towards Lower Berry Hill; where a right-hand turn at New Inn leads to the Camp Site.

Or take the A466 south from Monmouth for Tintern and the lower Wye Valley.

4(b) VIA CHEPSTOW

Take the main trunk road A48 up the north bank of the Severn. From Chepstow, A466 runs north up the Wye Valley. A48 continues through Lydney to Gloucester; many byways through Dean Forest diverge from it, by left-hand turns, towards the north.

Bus services

Frequent motor-bus services follow the main roads, and full details may be obtained from Red-and-White Services Ltd., of The Bulwark, Chepstow (telephone 2326). Long distance buses operate from Chepstow, Lydney, and Gloucester to Swansea, Cardiff, and London, with connections at Cheltenham to most parts of England. Other long distance services link Monmouth, Cinderford and Ross with Swansea, Cheltenham and London, etc. Details are given in the *Associated Motorways* timetable, from Red-and-White Services, Ltd., The Bulwark, Chepstow.

Rail routes

The Western Region of British Railways operates train services to, but not into, the Forest Park. From most parts of the country the usual rail route runs through Gloucester. From Bristol and the southwest the quickest access is by the four-mile tunnel to Severn Tunnel Junction or Newport, both south-west of Chepstow; a change of train is necessary at one of these stations. From these stations and also from South Wales there are occasional trains to Chepstow and Lydney.

None of the railways actually within the Forest Park are now open to passenger traffic, but the following line on its fringes is still in operation:

Western Region, Gloucester–Lydney–Chepstow–Newport–Cardiff.

Ferries

A public passenger ferry operates in daylight hours across the Wye between Symonds Yat East and Symonds Yat West.

Ancient Monuments

Amongst the more important are:

GOODRICH CASTLE. Situated just north of the Forest Park and reached by crossing the Wye by Huntsham Bridge or Kerne Bridge.

TINTERN ABBEY. Cistercian, fourteenth century. Open daily except Christmas Day, from 9 to 4 in winter, 9 to 7 in summer; Sundays 12 to 4 in winter, 12 to 5 in summer.

CHEPSTOW CASTLE. Twelfth century stronghold of Marcher barons. Open daily.

OFFA'S DYKE. Saxon Earthwork. May be traced at several points on east bank of the River Wye. Its course is followed by the Offa's Dyke footpath, which follows the Welsh border from Chepstow northwards to Prestatyn.

ROMAN ROAD. From Lydney to Mitcheldean. Best seen near Blackpool Bridge, on the Blakeney-Parkend road.

CAERWENT. Roman camp of Venta Silurum, six miles south-west of Chepstow. Admission is free of charge. The modern village is on the actual site of the camp, but the main road to Newport now avoids it. A fine hoard of Roman remains from this camp may now be seen in the Newport Museum and Art Gallery.

ST. BRIAVELS CASTLE. Twelfth century, not open except as a Youth Hostel.

Amongst the finest *Churches* are those of Staunton, St. Briavels, Newland, Mitcheldean, and Ross-on-Wye.

Monmouth has its castle, a fine old bridge and gatehouse, and the Llangattock Collection of relics of Admiral Nelson.

Within easy reach of the Park are Gloucester Cathedral, Tewkesbury Abbey, Caldicot Castle, the ruined castles of Raglan, Grosmont, and Skenfrith and the Roman amphitheatre of Caerleon near Newport.

Viewpoints

These are so numerous that it is only possible to mention the more outstanding:

Bream War Memorial.

Buckstone, ½ *mile south west of Staunton, between Monmouth and Coleford* (plate 50).

Symonds Yat, *on the direct road from Coleford to Goodrich, two miles north of Christchurch Camp Site* (plates 14 and 15).

Dean Hill *or* Pleasant Style, *one mile west of Newham* (plate 20).

Mount-Pleasant, *just south of Cinderford on the road to Littledean.*

Ruardean Hill *by the road from Ruardean to Cinderford, 932 ft. high.*

Plump Hill, *one mile south of Mitcheldean on the Monmouth–Gloucester road, with a grand outlook towards the Cotswold Hills* (plate 51).

Tidenham Chase, *midway between Chepstow and St. Briavels, on the high road. Eastwards over the Severn.*

Wintour's Leap, *two miles north of Chepstow on the road to St. Briavels.*

There are also fine views west over the Wye from points near St. Briavels, and east over the Severn from the hills fringing the Newnham–Chepstow road, whilst the northern fringe of the Forest affords magnificent views of the Black Mountains of Breconshire, the plains of Herefordshire, and the Malvern Hills. Two particularly good viewpoints here are the picnic sites at Carter's Piece and Ready Penny.

In Tintern Forest the finest views east across the Wye are those from the Wind Cliff (plate 28) and the White Stone.

Prehistoric earthworks

A fine example of an early hill-fort stands on Welshbury Hill, 1½ miles north of Littledean; it lies within Welshbury Wood, which is owned by the Forestry Commission and can be approached by a steep uphill path from the Abenhall–Flaxley road.

The ramparts of another hill stronghold can be seen in the woods just south of the Symonds Yat car park, by following the waymarked path south.

A smaller but interesting old camp occurs near the school at Soudley.

Some place names in the Park

Blakeney: *Blacken* in 1185 A.D.; Black Island.
Chepstow: from the Anglo-Saxon *ceap*, a market, and *stow*, a town.
Cinderford: *Sinderford* in 950. *Sinder* was Old English for cinders or dross.
Clanna: See 'Glanau'.
Glanau: Welsh for 'hillsides'.
Lydney: *Lidaneg* in 972; the Broad Island.
Meend: From Welsh *mynydd*, mountain.
Monmouth: stands where the River Monnow joins the Wye.
Newnham: called *Nevneham* in Domesday Book, is simply the new *ham* or village.
Ross: from Welsh *rhos*, a steep hill or promontory.
Symonds Yat: Yat is believed to be a corruption of *geat*, or gate, a term used where a trackway crosses a boundary.

There is a hint of Scandinavian influence in some of the local names, arising perhaps from the Vikings who sailed up the Severn Sea. The 'hopes' of Longhope and Cannop (Can-hope) recall Norse *hopr*=valley. The 'ey' of Lydney and Blakeney is the Norse *oy* meaning island. Several 'slades' recall *slettr*—flat land on a valley bottom; while the hilltop 'edges' stem from the Norse *egg*. A 'riding' and 'Reddings Enclosure', show a link with Norse *rydning*, a clearing, while those 'hams', which are flat stretches of land beside the Severn, represent the Norse *holm*, and not the Saxon *ham*, which is a village homestead.

The alder tree has a remarkable local name in the Dean. It is called the 'orrell tree', apparently a compound of the Norse *or* and the Danish *el*.

Though it is generally agreed that the name *Forest of Dean* arises from the many *denes* or wooded valleys, the alternative derivation 'forest of *Danes*', is not without some foundation.

West of the Wye the older place names are nearly all Welsh, and a sprinkling of Welsh names, such as the 'meends', persists in the Dean.

Only along the Severn plain are the 'tons', 'hams', and 'leys' of the Anglo-Saxon firmly established.

Fishing

The salmon fishing in the Wye is preserved, but coarse fishing for grayling, pike, chub, dace, perch, roach and eels is available for the visitor. Wye Board Licences may be obtained from the Wye River Board Fishery Office, Wilson's Chambers, Commercial Street, Hereford, or local distributors. In addition, the permission of local owners is required to fish their waters; such permits are obtainable from the Hereford Angling Association, the Ross Angling Association, and the Royal Hotel, Symonds Yat.

The Forest of Dean Angling Club looks after pond fishing within the Forest bounds.

Cars in the Forest: the Scenic Drive

The motorist is welcomed in the Forest of Dean because it is fast becoming an area of recreation in which the motor car acts as the "conveyor" of people seeking leisure and pleasure away from the home and work surroundings.

A scenic drive route opened in 1969 has become very popular, consisting of twenty five miles of County Council tarmacadamed roads linking some of the historical and other beautiful parts of the Forest of Dean. Based as a tour with the day visitor in mind but also catering for the holiday maker, it can be joined in many places and is well sign posted at road junctions.

The covering map and notes of the drive can be purchased everywhere that the other local Forestry Commission publications can be

St. Briavel's Castle

obtained. The map is designed to show a visitor the main points of interest within as well as outside the bounds of the Forestry Commission, the notes offer a self conducted history and archaeological tour of places of interest on the Scenic Drive itself. Nearly all the Nature Trails of the forest can be found starting from points on the Scenic Drive. These trails enable the visitor to spend an enjoyable hour or two walking the woods on a circular route of normally two to three miles in length. At each of the trail starts, there is a car park and often an area set aside for picnics. The larger car parks-cum-picnic areas have toilet facilities as well with areas for children to have a ball game as a break from the monotony of travelling on the back seat of the car.

No private cars are allowed to use the *Forestry Commission roads* except on business or as access to picnic sites and camping grounds.

The sporting aspect of motoring is catered for in the field of car rallying; where, in common with other forests in the country, car rallies to a maximum of four in any twelve months can pass through. Such rallies organised by clubs affiliated to the Royal Automobile Club pay a fixed rate per mile per car for every car that starts on the rally. Local club members therefore who pay to gain experience in this sport may go on to perform for British manufacturers in International car rallies in Europe and throughout the World.

Riding in the Forest

Riding is becoming a popular pastime in the forest as it lends itself to this form of recreation. There are several local stables, which have horses and ponies for hire; from where the rider can depart on his or her journey along well defined paths and disused railway lines catching glimpses of the rugged Welsh Mountains or the Severn Vale and Cotswold plateau. The route the rider follows has been designed to cover as much of the forest as possible giving a wide variety of surfaces to aid both rider and horse.

There are riding establishments scattered around the forest which provide well trained friendly horses and ponies for novice and advanced riders, beginners are also welcome. Ponies are for hire by the hour or day trekking parties. Riding holidays are arranged, where the riders have the choice of staying at one of the well-appointed camps or accommodation as otherwise arranged at local hotels or private houses.

Every opportunity exists for complete training of horse and riders which includes equitation and horsemanship for Pony Club or Riding Club tests including dressage up to British Horse Society standards, these lessons are by appointment.

For people with their own horses—don't leave them at home, bring them with you on holiday—stabling is available with either full livery or do-it-yourself feeding and grooming. Hunting is also arranged either in the forest or surrounding country.

If parents are not riders the Forest is an ideal centre for touring and walking, excellent wayside inns for midday refreshments. See the wild fallow deer in their natural surrounds and lots of other wild life, when walking or riding.

There is a Forest of Dean riding club, where riding and training can be enjoyed in the company of other interested people, particulars of a marked riding route, and details of the other services available can be had from the Forestry Commission, Crown Offices, Coleford or the Camp Office, Christchurch Camp Site, Coleford, Gloucester.

Locally produced guides to forest trails, etc.

Centres where guides are available are situated at Coleford (Crown Offices), Cinderford, Lydney, Ross-on-Wye, Tintern, Chepstow and Symonds Yat. Besides the guides to the Forest Walks listed below, the following publications are also available:

Dean, Visitor Map, 10p;
Dean Forest and Wye Valley, Short Guide, 4p;
A Scenic Motor Drive through the Dean Forest Park, 10p;
Geology of Symonds Yat and Wye Gorge, 5p.

The Forest Trails

Biblins Adventure Trail, so/540153, 4p.
Boys Grave & Cannop Ponds, so/607100, 4p.
Christchurch Trail, so/569179, 4p.
Parkend Forester School Trail, so/621081, 4p.
Speech House Trail, so/620121, 4p.
Symonds Yat, so/562160, 5p.
Wye Valley Geological, so/562160, 5p.
Wilderness Countryside Trail, so/659169, 5p.
Edge End Forest Walk, so/595136, 4p.
Abbotts Wood Forest Walk, so/659109, 4p.

Tintern Forest Trails

st/525970, 4m North of Chepstow on A466. 5p.
st/524004 and 526000 nearby.

Picnic places—Dean Forest

Speech House. so/623122, on B4220 2½m west of Cinderford.
Edge End. so/596134, on A4136 near its junction with B4028, 2m north-east of Coleford.
Beechenhurst. so/616119, on B4220 just east of Cannop.
Ready Penny. so/565148, on B4432 Coleford-Symonds Yat road ¾m south of Symonds Yat.
Cannop Ponds. so/608105, ¾m south of Cannop.
Boys Grave. so/622111, on by-road running south from B4220, 1m east of Cannop.
Knockley. so/607075, on by-road ¾m south-west of Parkend.
Wench Ford. so/654086, on B4431, 1½m north-west of Blakeney.

Mirey Stocks. so/614146, 3½m north-east of Coleford on B4028,
    near junction with B4234.
Information boards and maps are displayed at six of the picnic sites listed above.

Tintern

st/499984, of B4293 north from Chepstow to Devauden.
st/523028, near Ninewells, on by-road 1½m north of Tintern Parva.

Printed in Great Britain for Her Majesty's Stationery Office by Wells KPL Swindon Press
Dd 505979 K144 12/73

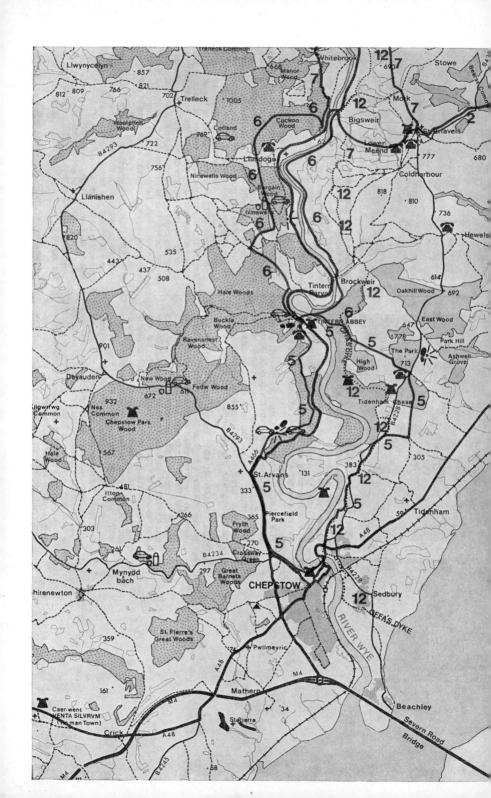